C.A. Meier

HEALING DREAM AND RITUAL

Ancient Incubation and Modern Psychotherapy

C.A. Meier

HEALING DREAM AND RITUAL

Ancient Incubation and Modern Psychotherapy

DAIMON
VERLAG

This book is an English translation of the German language work, *Der Traum als Medizin* (Daimon Verlag, Einsiedeln, 1985), which itself grew out of an earlier work by C.A. Meier entitled, *Antike Inkubation und moderne Psychotherapie* (Rascher, Zürich, 1949). This earlier German language work appeared in English translation in 1967 under the title, *Ancient Incubation and Modern Psychotherapy* (Northwestern University Press). The author was ably assisted in the work of translating and editing by David Roscoe, Gary Massey, John Peck, Liza Burr and Robert Hinshaw, and Liza Burr and John Peck compiled the Index for this volume. Mr. George Page is also hereby acknowledged with gratitude for helping to make this publication possible.

Healing Dream and Ritual by C.A. Meier,

First edition

Am Klosterplatz, CH-8840 Einsiedeln, Switzerland

ISBN 3-85630-510-6

Cover image: Asclepius, by Joel T. Miskin
Cover design: Joel T. Miskin, assisted by Hanspeter Kälin
Photo of C. A. Meier by Sam Francis

TABLE OF CONTENTS

INTRODUCTION

> [The doctor] ought to be able to bring about love and reconciliation between the most antithetic elements in the body.... Our ancestor Asclepius knew how to bring love and concord to these opposites, and he it was, as poets say and I believe, who founded our art.
>
> Plato, *Symposium* 186 D

OVER FIFTY YEARS AGO, while working in a psychiatric clinic, I became convinced of the need to study incubation in the ancient world. Material produced by psychotic patients seemed to contain symbols and motifs familiar to me from my scanty studies of ancient literature. Yet the content of this material showed quite plainly that, even in psychosis, which medical science usually approached in a defeatist spirit, there was a factor at work that we call today, rather inadequately, the "self-healing tendency of the psyche."

I found in C.G. Jung's analytical psychology a method by which I could observe those spontaneous healing processes at work. This is possible, however, only if the observer adopts a waiting attitude, letting the process happen, listening to it, as it were, and following it in all humility. This, in our modern therapeutic situation, would represent the *genius loci*. Further, analytical psychology, with its theory and the wealth of parallels it has collected from the history of religion and folk psychology, is an instrument that grants us deep insight into the psyche of sick mankind; with it, too, we can form a truer idea of the developmental processes in those whom we call healthy. Analytical psychology (research workers have already proven its usefulness in many studies in widely separated disciplines) can help us understand historical material previously misinterpreted or poorly explained.

Analytical psychology can help us, for example, to understand the problems a study of incubation raises. The ancient sources are available to us today, but the psychological aspect has been neglected. This is indeed regrettable, since Karl Kerényi's work has shown that the psychological approach is extremely fruitful when applied to Greek mythology and ritual. Here I wish to acknowledge my gratitude for the guidance gleaned from Kerényi's work and how stimulating his frequent and friendly conversations with me have been.

R. Herzog[1] spent many years studying Epidaurus and, more particularly, Cos. He has cleared up many points. Alice Walton[2] published a detailed study of Asclepius in 1894. Yet a more recent work on the subject, by the Edelsteins,[3] reveals the complete neglect of the psychological and, even more, comparative standpoint that has characterized all these works.

Since the incubation motif is eternal and ubiquitous, I shall confine myself in this study to material from classical antiquity. The material there is probably the least known, but that period offers everything necessary to an understanding of this subject. It is true that parallels to the healing miracles of Asclepius may be seen in the miraculous cures of the Church right down to the present day. This material, however, contains nothing that cannot be found in the ancient world. Indeed, it may even be more controversial. All that is important from our point of view is to note here that the Church follows very ancient paths and is continuing a great tradition. One thing more should be pointed out: the many similarities in the records of pagan and Christian miraculous cures are not due to imitation. This is sufficiently

1 R. Herzog, cf. below, pp. 10 and 13, Chap. I; n. 3, Chap. 2; n. 31, Chap. 3; and *WHE*.

2 Alice Walton, *The Cult of Asklepios*, Cornell Studies in Classical Philology No. 3 (New York, 1894).

3 Emma J. Edelstein and Ludwig Edelstein, *Asclepius* (2 vols.; Baltimore, 1945).

shown by the striking Indian parallels noted by Weinreich.[4] Other similarities are dealt with by Reitzenstein[5] and Deubner.[6]

According to the Samkhya doctrine, all the world's sickness and suffering are due to the body's contamination of the soul. These ills will therefore only disappear when "discriminating knowledge" – liberation of the soul from the physical world – is attained.[7] Thus, for example, we should not be surprised to find, in the final initiation rites of some Tibetan monks, a striking similarity to those employed in consulting the Trophonius oracle.[8]

As I have said, I shall, in this work, omit discussing these matters in detail, since the highly developed ancient rite and the discoveries of modern psychology alone enable us to understand incubation. These modern psychological discoveries are to be found in the works of C.G. Jung, so I shall avoid complicating this study by continual references to them.

The general attitude of mind toward dreams prevalent in the ancient world requires some explanation. Incubation's effectiveness is very closely bound up with the importance accorded to dreams. Only when dreams are very highly valued can they exert great influence. Büchsenschütz[9] has carefully assembled the source material concerning the opinions held on dreams in antiquity. Therefore, I need not try to assess them here. Only one last point need be emphasized: the Greeks, especially in the early period, regarded the dream as something that really happened; for them it was not, as it was in later times and to "modern man" in particular, an imaginary experience.[10] The natural consequence of this attitude was that people felt it necessary to create

4 O. Weinreich, *AHW*, pp. 176 f.

5 R. Reitzenstein, *Hellenistische Wundererzählungen* (Leipzig, 1906).

6 L. Deubner, *Kosmas und Damian: Texte und Einleitung* (Leipzig and Berlin, 1907).

7 Cf. Anandarayamakhi, *Das Glück des Lebens,* ed. A. Weckerling (Greifswald, 1937).

8 Cf. Alexandra David-Neel, *Mystiques et magiciens du Thibet* (Paris, 1929), pp. 210 ff.

9 B. Büchsenschütz, *Traum und Traumdeutung im Alterthume* (Berlin, 1868).

10 Cf. Roscher, *Lexikon,* III/2, 3203.

the conditions that caused dreams to happen. Incubation rites induced a *mantikē atechnos* (prophecy without system), an artificial *mania,* in which the soul spoke directly, or, in Latin, *divinat.*[11] In modern analytical psychology, too, we find what might be described as a method for constellating the natural "soothsaying" of the psyche.

If, as we put it today, the unconscious is to speak, the conscious must be silent. In antiquity the blind seer – Tiresias is the best known – was the fit embodiment of this idea.

The autonomous factor in the psyche revealed in such images and healing dreams surely merits our highest respect. Thus Aristotle[12] refers to incubation as a therapeutic method. In the book *On Diet* (Parva Naturalia),[13] Part IV, he develops a theory on the dream sent by a god. The Stoa developed this idea still further, and regarded healing dreams as an expression of divine *pronoia* ("foresight"). The later Academy and the Epicureans violently criticized this view, but with the Neo-Pythagoreans and the Neo-Platonists it was soon to reach a still higher culmination.

Studying the sources, we see at once that incubation is for the cure of bodily illnesses alone. You might then ask what it has to do with psychotherapy. In the first place, the sources constantly emphasize that Asclepius cares for *sōma kai psychē,* both body and mind – "body and soul" is the corresponding Christian term; and second, bodily sickness and psychic defect were for the ancient world an inseparable unity. The saying *mens sana in corpore sano,* which is often misunderstood today, is a later formulation of this idea.

Thus in antiquity the "symptom" is an expression of the *sympatheia,*[14] the *consensus,* the *cognatio* or *coniunctio naturae,* the point of correspondence between the outer and the inner. Stoic doctrine understood the concept in a very broad sense; it means the natural coincidence of particular phenomena, perhaps

11 Cicero *De divin.* ii. 26.
12 Aristotle, *Peri hierēs nousou.*
13 *Peri diaitēs.*
14 Cicero *De divin.* ii. 124.

even in different parts of the world; thus it corresponds to C.G. Jung's notion of synchronicity.

When, later, especially in the Empire, the incubants' dreams become healing oracles, which prescribe for the illness, the original concept of incubation begins to decay. The dream itself is no longer the cure. I have shown elsewhere[15] that this phenomenon of prescription by dream sometimes occurs even today; it, too, is psychologically interesting in connection herewith.

In what follows the reader should bear in mind one important archetypal theme constantly, namely, the myth of the night-sea-journey, first presented in complete form by Frobenius.[16] The links are particularly striking in connection with the oracle of Trophonius. Here a remark of Paracelsus may be apt; he says that in the belly of the whale Jonah saw the great mysteries.[17]

One other significant fact should be rescued from oblivion. The doctors of Attica were required to sacrifice publicly twice a year to Asclepius and Hygieia for themselves and their patients.[18]

Although it will be obvious to anyone acquainted with C.G. Jung's work how much his discoveries influence this study, I wish to emphasize it once again and express my deep gratitude to him.

C. A. MEIER

Rome
May 1948

Zürich
Fall 1988

15 C.A. Meier, "Chirurgie-Psychologie," *Schweiz. Med. Wschr.*, LXXIII (1943), 457 ff.
16 L. Frobenius, *Das Zeitalter des Sonnengottes* (Berlin, 1904).
17 Quoted from C.G. Jung, *Paracelsica* (Zürich, 1942), p. 101.
18 *IG*, II^2, No. 772.

CHAPTER I

THE DIVINE SICKNESS

THE QUESTION whether ancient prototypes of modern psychotherapy exist has never been fully investigated. Since, in antiquity, everything to do with the psyche was embedded in religion, it is necessary to look for these prototypes in ancient religion. The first definite clue I found was a passage in Galen, where this most famous physician of late antiquity proudly styles himself the "therapeut" of his "fatherly god, Asclepius."[1] What is the meaning of the word *therapeutēs*? It can only be the name originally given to those who were the attendants of the cult and who served the god by carrying out the prescribed ritual. From this point of view, therefore, *psychotherapists* would be people who were concerned with the cult of the psyche. Erwin Rohde,[2] in his still unsurpassed work *Psyche,* has shown how much the religions of antiquity were cults of the psyche, so that the spiritual welfare of anyone taking an active part in religious life was looked out for.

But what happened in case of sickness? Here I got a second reference through a dream dreamt by a woman patient at a critical phase of her treatment. It consisted of the laconic sentence:

I. "The best thing he created is Epidaurus."

As is usual with such "irrefutable assertions," no context was obtainable. I knew, however, that my patient had been in Greece, and I reminded her that there was a town of this name in

1 πάτριος θεὸς Ἀσκληπιὸς, Galen vi. 41 and xix. 19 (ed. Kühn). I am indebted to C.G. Jung for the information that in the Greek Patristic writings the monk is called θεραπευτής.

2 E. Rhode, *Psyche: Seelencult und Unsterblichkeitsglaube der Griechen* (2 vols.; Freiburg i.B., 1898).

Argolis. She thereupon remembered the theater – perhaps the finest of all ancient theaters[3] – which she had seen there, and slowly the recollection of the local Asclepian sanctuary, to which Epidaurus owes its fame, came back to her. Thus the appearance of the name in the dream was a sort of cryptomnesia.

Actually this dream prompted me to investigate the whole problem of incubation; and this study is really a somewhat detailed amplification of the key word "Epidaurus" appearing in the dream. Thus the riddle of Dream I should always be borne in mind. Some of the amplifications may seem very farfetched. But by bringing forward further material from daily psychotherapeutic practice, it can be shown that these ancient themes are still very much alive in the psyche of modern man. Knowledge of these themes is a valuable help to us for understanding modern problems. But our patients' problems are the problems of psychotherapy and therefore the psychotherapist's. Thus we are grateful for all clues to the traditional prototypes of our own activities. I find it very satisfying that many of these are in the "classical" field. I shall show that this exploration of antiquity will reward us with some unexpected glimpses into the "archaeology" of the human psyche. And, perhaps, the dusty records of the ancient world will take on a surprising new life, vividly illuminating many of the complex problems of modern psychotherapy and enhancing their interest.

Then from a study of what was practiced in the ancient Asclepieia, I was able to obtain an answer to my second question as to what was done in ancient times for the cult of the soul in the case of sickness. The answer was not, as we should be inclined to believe, ancient medicine or a physician, but exclusively a god or savior named Asclepius, not a human, but a divine physician. The reason for this was that classical man saw sickness as the effect of a divine action, which could be cured only by a god or another divine action.

Thus a clear form of homeopathy, the divine sickness being

3 Pausanias ii. 27. 5.

cast out by the divine remedy (*similia similibus curantur*), was practiced in the clinics of antiquity. When sickness is vested with such dignity, it has the inestimable advantage that it can be vested with a healing power. The *divina afflictio* then contains its own diagnosis, therapy, and prognosis, provided of course that the right attitude toward it is adopted. This right attitude was made possible by the cult, which simply consisted in leaving the entire art of healing to the divine physician. *He* was the sickness *and* the remedy. These two conceptions were identical. Because he was the sickness, he himself was afflicted (wounded or persecuted like Asclepius or Trophonius),[4] and because he was the divine patient he also knew the way to healing. To such a god the oracle of Apollo applies: "He who wounds also heals,"[5] *ho trōsas iasetai*.

The Asclepiads Machaon and Podalirius were unable to cure Telephus, wounded in the left thigh by Achilles. Achilles then received the oracle quoted above. Odysseus interpreted it thus: the remedy is the rust scraped from the point of Chiron's spear, with which Achilles had wounded Telephus. The fact that Telephus, poor and an outcast,[6] is compelled to seek refuge with his former enemies and finds healing there is a subtle psychological touch. Apuleius[7] also relates that Psyche had wounded herself with Cupid's arrow, bringing many sorrows on herself, but was healed by the selfsame arrow. Her healing begins with a catabasis[8] followed by an anabasis, her apotheosis (night-sea-journey). We shall encounter this mythological situation again in connection with several other healing divinities or heroes. These exam-

4 Trophonius: (*a*) swallowed up by the earth when fleeing from Augias, Apostolius 6. 82, quoted from Gruppe in Roscher, *Lexikon*, V, 1268; (*b*) starved, Scholiast on Aristophanes *Clouds* 508. Further to this theme cf. also in Roscher, *Lexikon, s.v.* "Melampus" and "Iphikles," 2570.

5 Apollodorus *Epit.* 3. 20: ὅταν ὁ τρώσας ἰατρὸς γένηται: he will not be healed "before he who wounded him becomes a doctor." Cf. also Suetonius, Claud. 93, and J.G. Graevii, *Suetonius Tranquillus, Claudius 43* (Trajecti ad Rhenum, 1673), p. 520, with his scholia.

6 *pauper et exul,* Horace *Ars Poetica* 96.

7 Apuleius *Metamorphoses* iv. 28-vi. 24.

8 εἰς Ἅιδου

ples belong to a widespread mythological theme also used by Goethe[9] and Richard Wagner.[10]

Hercules is another sick and suffering healing hero who sends disease. He is therefore able to heal sickness. He suffered from epilepsy, *morbus sacer*. He was called *alexikakos* ("averter of evil") because he averted an epidemic of the plague, and *sōtēr* ("savior") because he freed the land from another epidemic. This may explain why the Coan Asclepiads always boasted of their descent, on the paternal side from Asclepius, but on the distaff from Hercules.[11]

This mythological theme is an ancient prototype of the modern requirement that every analyst should undergo a training analysis; although it would be wrong to suppose that a training analysis is *nothing but* educational.

The myth of the ambivalent *pharmakon,* drug, always poison and antidote at the same time, is also found in the unconscious of

9 Goethe, *Tasso,* IV. iv:

> Die Dichter sagen uns von einem Speer,
> Der eine Wunde, die er selbst geschlagen,
> Durch freundliche Berührung heilen konnte.

("The poets tell of a spear which could heal with a friendly touch a wound which it had itself inflicted.")
The same "motive" can already be found in the libretto of the first opera in the history of music, *Il Ritorno d'Ulisse in Patria,* by Monteverdi.
The text is the work of the Venetian nobleman Giacomo Badoaro (Venice, 1641). Pisandro sings in Act II:

> Amor, se fosti arciero in saettarmi
> or da forza a quest' armi
> che vincendo dirò:
> se un arco mi ferì,
> un arco mi sanò.

("Love, you played the archer in shooting me. Now give strength to my arm so that I may say in winning that if a bow has wounded me a bow has also cured me.") Petrarch is also familiar with this "motive," as can be seen in his "Rime" 164 (9-11):

> Cosi sol d'una chiara fonte viva
> move 'l dolce e l'amaro, ond'io mi pasco;
> una man sola mi risana e punge.

10 Richard Wagner, *Parsifal,* III. ii: "Die Wunde schließt der Speer nur, der sie schlug." ("The wound can only be healed by the spear which inflicted it.")

11 R. Herzog, *Koische Forschungen und Funde* (Leipzig, 1899).

modern man. The following fantasy of a woman patient is an example:

II. I was on a level plain beside the sea. A man made of fire came dancing toward me. He was dancing to music from an unseen source, and he asked me to dance with him. I danced for a long time with my fiery partner without getting tired and without catching fire. We came to a tree and danced round it. Once I looked up and saw a tiger looking down at us with flashing eyes. The animal frightened me. But the fiery man just touched the tree, which burst into flame. The tree and the tiger were burnt up. We continued dancing round the fire until it went out and nothing was left but a heap of smoking ashes. I raked through them and found a lump of gold, which I took with me.

The fiery man then danced down to the sea, and I followed him, fascinated by the strange sight. He went onto the water. I hesitated to go after him, but he beckoned to me more and more urgently. At last I followed him there, too. At first we moved easily over the waves, but then there came a great wave which broke over us, and we both sank down into the depths. The fiery man still shone even under the water. Then there came a great and terrible fish, with sharp teeth, which swallowed us both. It was not dark in its belly, because the fiery man gave out a bright light. I was hungry and exhausted, so I cut off a piece of the fish's heart and ate it. This strengthened me greatly. My partner now set the fish alight with his fire, so that it was convulsed with pain and spewed us out. Then we sank down still deeper, leaving the burning fish behind us, until we came to the bottom of the sea. There the man led me to a *spring* of poisonous green water, and asked me to stop it up with my lump of gold because it was *poisoning* the whole sea. He said it was not good for the water to stream out into the sea and not onto the land. Combined with the sea water it turned to poison, whereas on land it had been a

healing spring. For some reason, however, it had dried up there and was now flowing out into the sea. If it were stopped up here, it would probably once again find its original proper channel. It had formerly been the central point of a *temple,* and its water had healed many people.
After he told me this I went to the spring and stopped it up with the lump of gold. I managed this successfully, but in doing so I was poisoned by the water and could only go a few steps farther before I sank down. As I lay on my back, the fiery man came and thanked me for what I had done. Then he kissed me on the mouth, and I felt that his fire penetrated my body. In this way he put out his own fire and disappeared. But the fire burned up the poison in my body, and I was cured. It also gave me a strong upward impulse, so that I rose up to the surface of the sea. I swam to shore and went up a road; here I met people and spoke to them. When I spoke, fire came out of my mouth, and this set alight a fire in the other people, too, so that their eyes began to shine.
They told me that they were going to a nearby temple and that the healing spring in this temple was flowing again. When I heard this, I went there too, for the fire in me hurt, and I thought that the healing water might alleviate this pain.
When I came to the temple, I waited until evening, when no one else was there, and went in. It was the round temple with the twelve pillars which is golden inside,[12] and in the middle the water flowed out in the form of a small fountain. I drank a mouthful of it, and there was a violent hissing inside me; I was torn asunder into a thousand pieces, which were hurled against the walls of the temple, and I fell to the ground. Only my left eye did not remain inside the temple but was hurled out of an upper window with such great

12 The reference is to a temple of which the patient had previously made a clay model.

> impulse that it flew up to a star and remained hanging there. A belated visitor now entered the temple. It was a little old bent, black-clad woman. She limped and carried a basket on her arm. She gathered up into the basket all the fragments of me which were lying around the temple. While doing this she found a large pearl lying on the ground which had formed inside me when the water mingled with the fire. She put it in her dress pocket. Then she emptied the contents of her basket into the water and hobbled off. The healing power of the water, however, joined my torn body together again, so that, when day dawned, I once more stepped out whole from the water.

The rest of the fantasy deals with the reintegration of the eye. In the course of our inquiry we shall find this fantasy recurring in a number of forms paralleling those of antiquity.

The inner connection between the divine sickness and the divine physician formed the core of the art of healing in the ancient world. But ancient Greek scientific medicine was developing along with theurgic medicine. It was developed to combat disease. The disease was now separate from the physician himself. Hippocrates and Galen were the founders of this form of medicine. Oddly enough, however, the Hippocratic school of medicine at Cos could not refrain, after the death of its founder, from setting up an Asclepieium there, thus showing that in the long run it could not dispense with theurgic medicine.[13] Suffice it to say, a hundred years after the death of Hippocrates, the cult of Asclepius in Cos was the state cult and the serpent staff of Asclepius was the insignia of the city.[14] In Athens, too, as early as the fourth century B.C., the *archiatēr* (official physician) regarded the Asclepieium as his center.[15] Galen was better disposed toward Asclepius than Hippocrates had been. Galen came

13 Cf. pp. 127 ff.

14 R. Herzog, "Heilige Gesetze von Kos," pp. 39 ff., 46 ff.

15 F. Kutsch, *Attische Heilgötter und Heilheroen,* pp. 26, 59, No. 21; p. 65, No. 30 (*RGVV,* XII, 3 [1913]).

from Pergamum, which was second only to Epidaurus as the center of worship of the divine physician Asclepius, and that may account for his partiality. He received his philosophical and early medical training there. A dream of his father's[16] inspired Galen to become a physician. In a dream Asclepius also cured him of a mortal illness (an abscess).[17] Thus Galen, too, is an example of the doctor able to heal because of his own sickness. He also used dreams for diagnosis. It was probably owing to the influence of Pergamum that he strongly favored the patient's obeying the instructions of the gods rather than those of the doctors.[18] Also he carried out operations at the behest of dreams, *ex oneiratōn*.[19] It is true that his colleagues did likewise, but, as they were competitors, they did so *aischrōs*,[20] "unjustifiably." In general he let Asclepius advise him concerning treatment[21] and made use of this to strengthen the authority of his prescriptions with the patient. In extreme cases the god overcame the skepticism of patients by confirming Galen's prescriptions in their dreams.[22]

Hippocrates, too, in spite of his strictly scientific attitude, granted the divine element its place in the art of healing, for in his *Peri euschēmosynēs*[23] *(Concerning the Grace of Demeanor Which Is Required for the Profession of Medicine),* he says, *iētros gar philosophos isotheos* ("the physician who is also a philosopher is godlike").

This attribution of a divine quality to the physician is not without its dangers, for it exposes him to the risk of inflation; nevertheless, it is better than secularizing medicine altogether.

16 Galen xvi. 222 K.
17 *Ibid.* xix. 19 K.
18 *Ibid.* xvii. b 137.
19 *Ibid.* xvi. 222 K.
20 *Ibid.* xiv. 220 K.
21 *Ibid.* xi. 314 K.
22 *Ibid.* x. 972 K. (Cf. also Galen's work *Peri tēs ex enypniōn diagnōseōs:* "On the diagnosis resulting from dreams").
23 Hippocrates c. 5.

CHAPTER II
EPIDAURUS

In this section I shall return to Dream I. But before I do so, I should like to say that, in what follows, I intend to deal with the amplifications of the key word "Epidaurus." The meaning of very concise dreams like Dream I, where no subjective associations can be obtained and where the context is generally very scanty, can only be obtained through amplification. This means establishing the *objective* context. Here it meant collecting data about Epidaurus and finding their meaning. These amplifications, as I hope to demonstrate, throw light on the ancient cult of the psyche in its relation to illness and thus enable us to discover the ancient prototype of modern psychotherapy and what is today called psychosomatic medicine.

Epidauros Hiera, "Epidaurus the Holy," lies five miles inland from Epidaurus in the Argolid. It dates back to about the sixth century B.C. and remained active, with several successive periods of prosperity and decay, until the third century A.D. It consists of a sacred enclosure, *peribolos,* marked off with boundary stones.[1] The principal deity to whom it was sacred was Asclepius. The worship of Asclepius in other places did not die out until the fifth century A.D., so that probably his healing powers were exercised for more than a thousand years. Epidaurus was and continued to be the center of this god's cult, although later on every important city founded its own Asclepian sanctuary. Epidaurus showed great skill in making these new centers affiliated offshoots of its own by seeing that the rite of "translation"[2] was strictly observed. According to Herzog,[3] Asclepius was

1 Pausanias ii. 27. 1.

2 The solemn transferral of the relics of a saint to another place (in Catholicism); the general ritual of the transfer.

3 Herzog, *WHE,* pp. 37 f.

introduced into Sicyon later than 480 B.C. The legend of the establishment of the cult has been handed down to us by Pausanias.[4] The god made his entry into Athens in 420 B.C. The legend of the establishment of his cult there will be dealt with later. The sanctuary at Pergamum, which was later to outstrip Epidaurus in fame and splendor, dates back to the first half of the fourth century B.C. This legend, too, is to be found in Pausanias.[5] Unfortunately, we have only a preliminary report on the excavations that have been conducted there.[6]

A legend which gives a particularly fine example of the symbolism of miraculous healing is to be found in Pausanias' account[7] of the founding of the sanctuary at Naupactus. The sanctuary was originally built by a private individual named Phalysius. When his eyes were so diseased that he was almost blind, the god of Epidaurus commanded the poetess Anyte to go to him with a sealed letter. She thought that the command was only a dream; but it soon proved to be a reality, for she found a sealed letter in her hand. She therefore sailed to Naupactus and asked Phalysius to open the letter and read what was in it. Phalysius thought he would not be able to read the letter, in view of the condition of his eyes. But, hoping for the favor of Asclepius, he broke the seal, and when he looked at the wax tablet he was cured. He then gave Anyte what the letter demanded: the sum of two thousand gold staters.

The transfer (*translatio*) of the cult to a new locality was almost always effected by transporting one of the sacred serpents to it, i.e., the god in his theriomorphic form, from the *hieron* ("sanctuary") at Epidaurus. The sanctuaries at Halieis,[8] Sicyon,[9]

4 Pausanias ii. 10. 3
5 *Ibid.* ii. 26. 8.
6 Otfried Deubner, *Das Asklepieion von Pergamon* (Berlin, 1938). Today, however, there are more detailed archaeological findings at our disposal in the shape of vol. 8, part 3, II, parts 1-4 of "Die Altertümer von Pergamon," ed. Deutsches Archäolog. Institut (Berlin, 1968-84).
7 Pausanias x. 38. 7.
8 *IG,* IV, 952, pp. 69 ff.
9 Pausanias ii. 10. 3; iv. 4. 7 and 14. 8.

and Epidaurus Limera were established in this way. Regarding the founding of the last-named sanctuary, which took place toward the end of the fourth century B.C., Pausanias writes:[10]

> The inhabitants say that they are not Lacedaemonians but Epidaurians from the Argolid. They had been sent by the city to Cos to consult Asclepius, and they landed at this point in Laconia. Here a dream was sent to them. They also say they brought a serpent with them from their home in Epidaurus. It escaped from the ship and disappeared into the earth on the shore. Therefore, in view of the visions in their dreams and of the omen of the serpent, they decided to settle down and live there. Where the serpent disappeared into the earth, there are the altars to Asclepius, with olive trees growing round them.

The Attic sanctuary was also founded in this way.[11] It is quite clear that the introduction of Asclepius into Athens at the end of the fifth century B.C. was soon followed by the elevation of his worship to the status of a state cult; it was also given the sanction of Delphi. Doubtless these events had a great deal to do with Asclepius' rapid Panhellenic deification.

The Asclepian sanctuary at Rome is perhaps the most famous example of translation from one precinct to another. Ernst Schmidt[12] has published a study on this. Ovid[13] and Livy[14] have also described the translation in detail.

Ovid reports that a terrible plague once raged in Latium, and all the art of the doctors was powerless against it. Then the inhabitants of the city made application to Delphi to beg for succor, but Apollo commanded them to seek nearer home, calling not upon him but upon his son. They learned that Apollo's son

10 *Ibid.* iii. 23. 4.
11 *Athen. Mitteil.*, XXI (1896), 314 ff.
12 Schmidt, "Kultübertragungen," *RGVV*, VIII, 2 (1910).
13 Ovid *Metamorphoses* xv. 622-744.
14 Livy x. 47. 6 ff.

had his home in Epidaurus, so they sent ambassadors there. They asked that the god Asclepius be handed over to them. This the Epidaurians were unwilling to do. During the night, however, Asclepius himself appeared to one of the Romans in a dream – in the form in which he was represented in the temple, the serpent-wreathed staff in his left hand and stroking his beard with his right – and told him that he would go with them to Rome. He would transform himself into a serpent, but it would be a very great one. Thus it happened on the following day, when they came to the temple. The earth quaked, and the god entered into the serpent. The huge creature went over flower-strewn roads through the middle of the city to the port and went on board the Roman vessel. Italy was reached in six days. The ship sailed along the coast until it reached Antium. A great storm was raging, and the god sought refuge in the temple of Apollo which stands on the shore. When the storm had abated, he returned to the ship, which proceeded to Ostia. Here he was greeted by the vestal virgins and the whole population. While the

---

Plate 1
View of Tiber Island by Antonio Lafreri (ca. 1573-77) in "Speculum Romanae Magnificentiae." Idealized representation with the four case histories (Greek) from the Asclepieium there.
The copper engravings published by Antonio Lafreri and his successors (Duchet, Nobili, Orlandi, van Schoel, Rossi) are closely linked to the scholarly and artistic interest shown in Rome in matters of antiquity. The engravings vividly capture this avid interest.
The tradition can be traced back to Leo X and research carried out by Raphael (engravings of M. Antonio Raimondi). After the "Sacco" there was a strong emphasis on urban architecture, when Sixtus V gave Dom Fontana the task of transforming the hitherto chaotic Rome into a splendid Baroque city, with broad streets lined with houses and with obelisks as signposts at the end of each street. Fontana himself took an active interest in antiquity. Lafreri also published other inscriptions in copper engravings, so there was nothing actually unusual about the publication of the Greek texts. It would nevertheless be interesting to find out *where* this text was at the time, and *when* it was discovered or its relationship with Tiber Island established. In the circles involved it was bound to have been regarded as a major event at the time.
Huelsen estimates that the Tiber Island engraving (edition A) was done in Lafreri's last years, i.e., between 1573 and 1577 – Lafreri died in July 1577. Huelsen writes, "Greek inscription from the Sclepius temple (1 gr. XLV 966)."

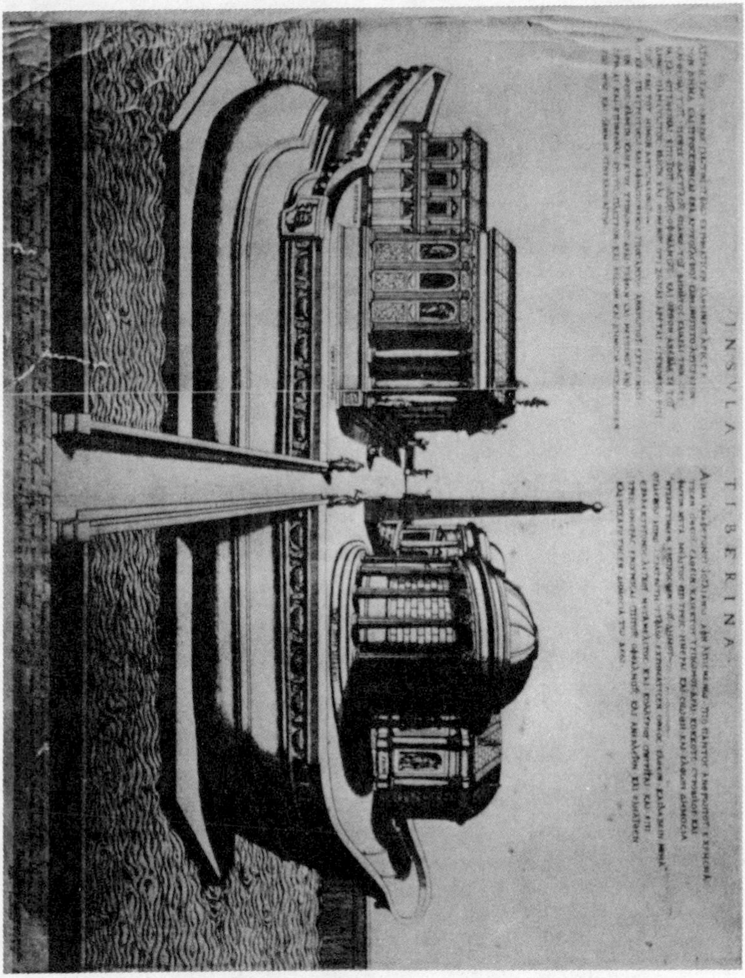
INSVLA TIBERINA

Plate 2
Roman mosaic in the Museum of Cos. (Photo by Marie Lene Putscher, Cologne.)
The rumor that the Hippocratic doctors of Cos reverted to the Asclepian medicine after the death of their hero, Eponymos, is confirmed in an amusing way through the archaeological find of a Roman floor mosaic from the 3rd century, undoubtedly based upon an older Greek portrait, depicting Asclepius' landing on Cos by boat and being received by a pensive Hippocrates.

ship was being drawn up the Tiber, the altars on both banks smoked with incense, and animals were sacrificed in honor of the god. As soon as they arrived at Rome, the god left the ship and went on to Tiber Island, where he resumed his divine form. With his arrival the plague ceased.

A sanctuary was established on Tiber Island in 291 B.C., and the island itself was later enclosed with slabs of travertine in the shape of the bows of a ship, which can still be seen. On them there is a carving of Asclepius and the serpent staff. An obelisk erected in the middle of the island represented the ship's mast; it has now disappeared. The famous hospital of the Fatebenefratelli now stands on the site of the Asclepieium. In the Church of San Bartolomeo, which is part of this hospital, the pillars come from the ancient temple of Asclepius. The altar steps lead down to a well of underground water from the Tiber.[15] The translation and establishment of a new sanctuary were for the most part undertaken at the instance of dreams or else, as in the case of Rome, after consultation of the Sybilline books. From the sanctuary on Tiber Island we have four inscriptive case histories (Greek), all of them completely in the style of the Iamata (healings) of Epidaurus. They are the so-called Maffei inscriptions. The stele itself has been lost, but its text, albeit incomplete, can be found in Besnier (p. 214/215) and also in Deubner (p. 44/45). It gives me great pleasure to be able to point out that the complete text can be read on a copper engraving by Antonio Lafreri (ca. 1575): "Insula Tiberina" in the "Speculum Romanae Magnificentiae" (see Fig. 110 C, e) in Christian Huelsen, "Das Speculum Romanae Magnificentiae," Catalogue of the works of Antonio Lafreri, under A: Continuation of the Speculum. 1: From Lafreri's last years (1573-77). Weinreich, in *RGVV* VIII/l, refers to these texts, too (cf. Plate 1).

Cos alone, with its *medical* school, characteristically rejected affiliation with Epidaurus. Yet the Coan sanctuary survived the

15 Cf. Mary Hamilton, *Incubation* (London, 1906), pp. 64 f., and M. Besnier, *L' Ile Tibérine dans l'antiquité* (Paris, 1902).

famous Coan school of medicine by at least two hundred years. Herzog[16] emphasizes that the alleged connection of Hippocrates with the Coan sanctuary, the Cyparissus (the main authority for which is the *Letters of Hippocrates*), is a legend of the Coan school of medicine. It cannot be correct because a sanctuary was not founded until the middle of the fourth century B.C. – that is, after the death of Hippocrates. The rumor claiming that after the death of their hero, Eponymus, the Hippocratic doctors on Cos resorted once more to Asclepian medicine is given amusing archaeological confirmation by a third-century Roman floor mosaic found there. There can be no doubt that this mosaic can be traced back to a Greek painting depicting Asclepius disembarking at Cos and being received by a somewhat pensive Hippocrates. Today the mosaic can be seen in the Museum of Cos (see Plate 2, photo taken by Professor Marie Lene Putscher, Cologne). Thus the legend that he is connected with it is a piece of *esprit d'escalier*. What carries it still further is that, as late as the fourteenth century A.D., Asclepius can be traced on the island of Cos in the form of a dragon, according to Herzog.[17] The legend is to be found in Sir John Mandeville's *Travels*.[18]

> And then pass men through the isles of Cophos and of Lango, of the which Ypocras was lord of. And some men say that in the isle of Lango is yet the daughter of Ypocras, in form and likeness of a great dragon, that is a hundred fathom of length, as men say, for I have not seen her. And they of the isles call her Lady of the Land. And she lieth in an old castle, in a cave, and sheweth twice or thrice in the year, and she doth no harm to no man, but if men do her harm. And she was thus changed and transformed, from a fair damosel, into likeness of a dragon, by a goddess that was clept Diana. And men say that she shall so endure in

16 Herzog, *Kos,* p. xi.
17 *Ibid.*, p. xiii.
18 *The Travels of Sir John Mandeville* (London: Library of English Classics, 1900), p. 17.

> that form of a dragon, unto [the] time that a knight come, that is so hardy, that dare come to her and kiss her on the mouth; and then shall she turn again to her own kind, and be a woman again, but after that she shall not live long.

The legend shows how much in need of redemption was the *anima* of Hippocrates with his hybrid background. The legend moves on from Cos to Rhodes.[19] Today the ruins of a Christian church of the Panagia Tarsou, "The Virgin," occupy the site of the Asclepian cypress grove, *to Alsos,* at Cos.

According to Herzog, the first, modest altar to Asclepius and his family at Cos was set up in the cypress grove there about the middle of the fourth century B.C., and his first temple, also a modest one, between 300 and 270 B.C. It was not until the middle of the fourth century B.C. – when the Hellenistic age was beginning – that a public cult of Asclepius was to be found at Cos. Here Epione was the wife of Asclepius and the daughter of Hercules.[20] Surprisingly enough, the sanctuary at Cos is the only one where, according to the inscriptions,[21] Asclepius is placed above his father, Apollo. From the psychological point of view, however, this is quite understandable as a necessary phenomenon of compensation for the low esteem in which Asclepius was traditionally held at Cos.

According to Thrämer[22] there were in the whole of the ancient world about 410 Asclepian sanctuaries, almost all of which were linked to Epidaurus.

19 Karl Herquet, "Der Kern der rhodischen Drachensage," *Wochenblatt des Johanniterordens Balley,* Brandenburg, X (1869), 151 ff.

20 Cf. above, p. 4.

21 Herzog, "Heilige Gesetze von Kos."

22 Thrämer, in Hastings, *ERE,* VI, 550.

CHAPTER III

ASCLEPIUS

> You must know, however, that Hercules, the Dioscuri, and Asclepius, and all the others who were begotten by the gods, went through labors and the self-controlled endurance of suffering before they finally found the blessed way to the gods. For the ascent to God is not given to men who have lived self-indulgently, but to those who have learned to endure courageously even in most difficult circumstances.
>
> Porphyrius, *Epistula ad Marcellam* 7

In this chapter I do not intend to give a comprehensive picture of Asclepius. Only those features and aspects important to our particular discussion will be mentioned.

Asclepius was originally a pre-Greek god, or rather demon, which may be seen from old forms of his name: Aischlabios, Aislapios, and so on. The most ancient center of the cult of Asclepius, unfortunately only poorly excavated, was probably Tricca in Thessaly. Strabo[1] calls it "the most ancient and famous sanctuary of Asclepius." There Asclepius was consulted as an oracle. He was thus definitely both mantic and chthonic in character. This is also shown by his animal attributes, the serpent and the dog. Probably Asclepius took over the dog from his father Apollo – Apollo Maleatas – who was a mighty hunter and lover of dogs and whose sanctuary on the Cynortion at Epidaurus was called "Cyon" (dog).[2] Moreover, when the infant Asclepius was

1 τὸ ἱερὸν τοῦ Ἀσκληπιοῦ τὸ ἀρχαιότατον καὶ ἐπιφανέστατον, Strabo ix, p. 437.

2 Gruppe, *Handbuch*, p. 1247.

exposed, he was fed by a sheep dog, as we learn from Apollodorus Atheniensis[3] and Tertullian.[4]

It may not be superfluous to draw attention to the similarity with Zeus in this respect. Menander Rhetor calls Apollo "Cynegetes,"[5] and, according to Dionysius of Chalcis,[6] Apollo begat Telmissus in the form of a dog. Among Indo-Germanic peoples in general, dogs are regarded as guides into the other world. The reader will remember the sacrifice of a dog to the dead in the *Iliad*.[7] Obviously their ability to follow a trail and their intuitive nature make them specially suitable for this role. These are also qualities which characterize the good doctor. Dogs are connected with birth and death, as can be seen from the Roman goddess Genita Mana, to whom dogs were sacrificed.[8] The dog was sacred also to the jackal-headed Anubis of Egypt. Anubis was later assimilated to Hermes as psychopompos under the name Hermanubis.

The association of Asclepius with the snake will be discussed in greater detail later. At this point I would merely like to draw attention to the following:

The serpent, as well as being an attribute of Asclepius, is connected with Zeus, Sabazius, Helios, Demeter, Cora and Hecate and also even more specifically with hero figures.[9] The ancients explained its association with Asclepius by its keen sight and by its power of rejuvenating itself, that is, casting its skin, which symbolizes becoming free from illness.[10] Later we shall

3 Apollodorus Atheniensis, Frag. 138 (ed. Jacoby).
4 Tertullian *Ad. nat.* ii. 14.
5 In L. Spengel, *Rhetor. Gr.*, III, 442.
6 Dionysius of Chalcis, Frag. 4 (*Fragm. Hist. Gr.*, ed. Müller, IV, 394).
7 *Iliad* xxiii. 168 ff.
8 Birth and death are combined in her name. Cf. Herbert Scholz, *Der Hund in der griechisch-römischen Magie und Religion* (diss.; Berlin, 1937); C.N. Deedes, "The Oinochoe of Tragliatella," in *The Labyrinth*, ed. Hooke (London, 1935); C.A. Meier, "Spontanmanifestationen des kollektiven Unbewußten," *Zentralblatt für Psychotherapie*, XI (Leipzig, 1939), 297, 300.
9 Cf. E. Küster, "Die Schlange in der griechischen Kunst und Religion," *RGVV*, XIII, 2 (1913).
10 Scholiast on Aristophanes *Plut.* 733.

see that getting rid of illness is equivalent to "putting on the new man" (shedding the skin).

Euripides[11] calls the hydra, despite its definitely snakelike nature, "the hound of Lerna" – a sign that the snake and the dog belong together. Many other chthonic demons are represented in the shape of the serpent and the dog: the Erinyes, the Gorgon, Cerberus, Empusa and Scylla. Both animals also act as their attendants. This is true of Hades, the god of Sinope (Darzales, also known as Serapis), Hecate, Despoina of Lycosura and Asclepius. The serpent and the dog guard treasures, have mantic-medicinal powers,[12] and represent the souls of the dead, that is, heroes. Their identity and their power to cause and cure illness are very clearly expressed in the following modern dream of a doctor:

III. I was at an exhibition with my two sons. Suddenly one of them, who had stayed a little way behind, called out, "A snake!" He had vomited up a worm about eighteen inches long (like a snake), and pulled it out of his mouth, and was holding it in the middle with his right fist. He ran to me to show me the snake. It had the head of a miniature dog. I said to him that I too had once had a worm like that, and that it was a good thing when it came out.

Asclepius' chthonic nature meant he was always worshiped near springs and groves. On the island of Cos it was the grove of Apollo Cyparissius. According to Valerius Maximus[13] and Dio Cassius,[14] Turullius, one of Caesar's murderers, cut down this grove about 32 B.C. to build ships for the fleet of Antony and Cleopatra. Octavian had him executed for it.[15] The protection of

11 Euripides *Hercules* 420.
12 Herzog, "Aus dem Asklepieion von Kos," *Arch. Rel. Wiss.*, X (1907), 201-28, 400-415.
13 Valerius Maximus i. 1. 19.
14 Dio Cassius 51. 8. 2.
15 Herzog, *Kos.*

the grove is attested on Stelae 11 and 12.[16] Pausanias[17] is the authority for the existence of a cypress grove at Titane. At Pergamum the sanctuary stood in the famous Rufine grove. This grove took its name from L. Cuspius Pactumeius Rufus, the founder of the circular temple of Zeus-Asclepius. On account of the groves in the *temenos,* or sacred precinct, the latter received the name *alsos,* "grove," which was later used for the whole temple precinct. The connection of Asclepius with groves and springs recalls another god curiously resembling Christ, Mithras, who was also worshiped *inter nemora et fontes.*

Asclepius goes through an interesting metamorphosis in Greek mythology: he was at first a mortal physician, and still is in Homer,[18] who calls him *amymōn iētēr,* "the incomparable physician." He then became a chthonic oracular demon or hero, and later still an Apollonian deity. As might be expected from these fluctuations in the view which was held of him, the genealogy of Asclepius is variable and confusing.[19]

In Pindar's Third Pythian Ode,[20] Coronis is pregnant with Asclepius by Apollo. Since, however, she wishes to marry Ischys – presumably to legitimize her child – she is overtaken by the god's vengeance and slain. According to Apollodorus,[21] Apollo learns the news of the unfaithfulness of Coronis from a raven. Until then the ravens were white, but Apollo, angry at the evil tidings, turned them black. Ovid[22] tells us that, just before the death of Coronis on the funeral pyre, Apollo rescued his unborn son with a Caesarean section – this is the motif of the miraculous birth of the hero – and gave him to Chiron the centaur to bring up. Wilamowitz,[23] with reference to Apollo's rescuing

16 Herzog, "Heilige Gesetze von Kos."
17 Pausanias ii. 11. 16.
18 *Iliad* iv. 182, 193.
19 Emma J. Edelstein and Ludwig Edelstein, *Asclepius* (Baltimore, 1945), Vol. II.
20 Pindar *Pythian Odes* iii. 14-15.
21 Apollodorus, Frag. 138 (ed. Jacoby); Hyginus *Fab.* 202; Ovid *Metamorphoses* ii. 632.
22 Ovid *Metamorphoses* ii. 632.
23 Wilamowitz, "Isyllos von Epidauros," *Philolog. Untersuch.*, IX (1886), 20.

Plate 3
Marble statue of Asclepius, now in the Museo Nazionale Napoli, but which stood originally in the Asclepieium on Tiber Island, Rome (Alinari No. 11072).

his son, says, "He who sent death gave life," which recalls the motif "He who has wounded also heals."[24] In Pausanias[25] the infant Asclepius is rescued not by Apollo but by Hermes.

Asclepius finally developed into a "Christian deity or saint," if the expression may be permitted. This development is revealed by the almost word-for-word similarity between the accounts of miraculous cures at Asclepian sanctuaries and those at Christian healing shrines during the Middle Ages and in the legends of saints.[26] The impossibility and absurdity of the ancient cures in these accounts are even more marked in those of Christian miraculous cures.[27] The Emperor Julian the Apostate[28] quite clearly put Asclepius on a level with Christ. For him, in any case, the ancient god of healing was a "divine man," like Christ, as Kern[29] points out. This, however, takes us beyond our theme.

The dark demonic figure of Asclepius becomes in later sculptures a Zeus-like, bearded man, whose most conspicuous quality is *ēpiotēs,* gentleness. According to ancient etymology[30] this is shown in his name, Asclepius. In this form he is a true son of Apollo, who, as his father, bore in Pergamum the epithet *kalliteknos,*[31] "he with the excellent son," and in that capacity had a temple of his own there.

Asclepius, as we have seen, learned the art of healing from Chiron the centaur. Chiron was incurably wounded by the

24 ὁ τρώσας ἰάσεται.

25 Pausanias ii. 26. 6.

26 Cf. L. Deubner, *De Incubatione* (Leipzig, 1900) and *Kosmas und Damianus, Texte und Einleitung* (Leipzig and Berlin, 1907); E. Lucius, *Die Anfänge des Heiligenkults* (Tübingen, 1904); H. Delahaye, *Les Légendes hagiographiques* (Paris, 1927) and *Les recueils antiques de miracles des saintes,* Analecta Bollandiana 32 (1925), pp. 5-84, 305-25; H. Günter, *Die Christliche Legende des Abendlandes* (1910); and especially Herzog, *WHE,* which refers particularly to the books of miracles at the South German healing shrines.

27 Herzog, *WHE,* n. 32, pp. 82 f.

28 Cf. Georg Mau, *Die Religions-Philosophie Kaiser Julians* (Leipzig, 1908).

29 θεῖος ἀνήρ, Kern, *Religion,* II, 308, n. 3.

30 Plutarch *Dec. orat. vitae* viii. 845 B; Eustathius *Comm. ad Homeri Odysseam* ii 319; Cornutus *Theol. Graec. comp.* cap. 33.

31 Aristides *Oratio* xxxxviii B. 18.

poisoned arrows of Hercules. Thus, he is another healer who is himself in need of healing. The proverbial "Chironian wound" applies to him.[32] Welcker[33] makes an interesting observation on the centaur nature of Chiron:

> This picture (in the Vienna Dioscorides, fifth century) merits the following interpretation: that anagogically the practical side of medicine is to be understood by the irrational part of Chiron (the horse) and the scientific side by the human part.

Anagogical readings, especially in Greek rhetoric, are spiritual or allegorical interpretations. Therefore, medical practice would have an essential connection with the irrational. We may then say that what *works* in medicine is irrational. The horse, like the serpent and the dog, is a chthonic animal. Thus it can heal or ward off evil.[34] An Epidaurian cure[35] illustrates this principle: a cripple is healed because Asclepius in a dream circumambulates him three times in a horse-drawn chariot and then lets the horses trample on his paralyzed limbs.

Healing Hercules[36] and Philoctetes[37] proved dangerous for Asclepius, since the latter act decided the outcome of the Trojan War. Carried away by these great feats, Asclepius finally dared bring dead men back to life: Hippolytus and Glaucus.[38] Zeus obviously regarded these acts as an interference with the divine order of things. He therefore punished the presumptuous healer by slaying him with a thunderbolt.[39] Diodorus[40] and Ovid[41]

32 Χειρώνειον ἕλκος, Zenobius 6. 46.
33 F.G. Welcker, *Kleine Schriften* (Bonn, 1850), III, 17.
34 P. Stengel, *Archiv für Religionswissenschaft,* VIII (1905), 203 ff., and Rochholz, *Naturmythen* (1862), pp. 26 ff.
35 Miracle XXXVIII in Herzog, *WHE.*
36 Pausanias iii. 19. 7.
37 Sophocles *Philoctetes 1437-38.*
38 Apollodorus *Bibl.* iii. 10. 3, 9-10.
39 Hesiod, Frag. 125 (ed. Rzach); Philodemos of Gadara *De pietate* 17. 1.
40 Diodorus *Bibl. hist.* iv. 71. 1-4.
41 Ovid *Fasti* vi. 743-62.

relate this Promethean sin and the envy of the gods which it provoked. In Diodorus' account, Hades complained to Zeus that Asclepius had greatly lessened his sphere of authority by "healing" so many dead men. He requested Zeus to do something about it.

After his death Asclepius undoubtedly worked miracles as a hero. We need only remember that, in general, statues of heroes were regarded as having healing properties, for instance, those of the Corinthian general, Pelichus,[42] and Hippocrates.[43] Lucian[44] says that in Athens the statue of Xenos Iatros (the stranger as doctor) stood by the grave of the hero Toxaris. Even the statue of Alexander of Abonuteichos, which stood near his cenotaph in the marketplace, was miraculous.[45] Alexander called himself a pupil of Asclepius. Statues of this kind, but more often only their hands and fingers, were often gilded, just as are those of the miracle-working Panagia in modern Greece. Patients in analysis often carefully execute paintings of symbols, particularly effective for them, where gold plays a special part.

Because Zeus had slain his son, Apollo bore the father of the gods a grudge, so he slew the Cyclopes, who had forged the thunderbolts for Zeus.[46] To expiate this deed, Apollo received a severe penalty from Zeus. He had to serve the mortal Admetus for a certain length of time as a shepherd slave. Since Apollo was a twin himself, he caused the ewes to bear nothing but twins during this period.[47] Ovid[48] consoled Apollo for the death of his son Asclepius in a manner interesting to psychology:

> *Phoebe, querebaris: Deus est, placare parenti:*
> *propter te, fieri quod vetat, ipse facit.*

42 Lucian *Philopseudes* c. 18 ff.

43 *Ibid.* c. 21.

44 Lucian *Skythes* c. 2.

45 O. Weinreich, "Alexandros der Lügenprophet und seine Stellung in der Religiosität des 2. Jahrhunderts nach Christus," *Neue Jahrbücher,* XLVII (1921), 129-51.

46 Acusilaus, Frag. 18 (ed. Jacoby).

47 Apollodorus *Bibl.* iii. 10; Callimachus *Hymn IV to Apollo* 47-54.

48 Ovid *Fasti* vi. 761-62.

> Phoebus, thou didst complain. But Aesculapius is a god, be reconciled to thy parent: he did himself for thy sake what he forbids others to do. (translation by Sir J.G. Frazer)

For Asclepius, the distinction of so uncommon a death had an unexpectedly agreeable consequence: he himself was given a place among the gods.[49] Minucius Felix[50] says in so many words: "Aesculapius ut in deum surgat fulminatur" ("the apotheosis of Asclepius was effected by his being struck by lightning"); and Artemidorus[51] states: "For no one who is slain by a thunderbolt remains without fame. Thus he is also honored as a god." According to Pseudo-Eratosthenes[52] Asclepius was placed among the stars because he was struck by a thunderbolt. He was placed in the Ophiuchus constellation (Serpentarius, the Serpent-Bearer) owing to his theriomorphic aspect. According to the astral myths, help for those born under the brightest star in Serpentarius derives from the epiphany or power of Asclepius or Serapis (for the Egyptians and their astrologers saw the god of medicine in this constellation[53]). A mystical interpretation of the astral theosophists explains Ophiuchus as the second creation, because he wrestles with the serpent and thus announces the second creation as rebirth through Christ.[54] Those born under this star followed occupations connected with the divine physician whom it was supposed to represent: doctors, slaughterers of animals, botanists and skillful makers of salves.[55] Ophiuchus also gave protection against poison.[56] According to Aristotle[57]

49 E. Rhode, *Psyche* (1898), I, 320 ff.
50 Minucius Felix *Octavius* xxiii. 7.
51 οὐδεὶς γὰρ κεραυνωθεὶς ἄτιμός ἐστιν ὅπου γε καὶ ὡς θεὸς τιμᾶται, Artemidorus *Oneirocr.* ii. 9.
52 Pseudo-Eratosthenes *Catasterismi* i. 6.
53 Aristides *Hier. log.* 4.5. ff. (pp. 439 f. K).
54 Hippolytus *Refut. Omn. haeres.* 4. 48. 8 (ed. Wendland, p. 71, 23 ff.).
55 W. Gundel, "Neue astrologische Texte des Hermes Trismegistos," *Abh. Akad. Münch., Phil. Abt.*, N.F., XII (1936).
56 W. Gundel, *Sterne und Sternbilder im Glauben des Altertums und der Neuzeit* (Bonn and Leipzig, 1922), p. 337.
57 Aristotle *Peplus* (Frag. 20).

Asclepius' two sons, Podalirius and Machaon, were also apotheosized.

Apotheosis naturally enabled Asclepius, as a *god* of healing, to work miracles which were no longer tied to his physical presence or his active therapy. The *chthonii,* of course, are bound to their particular locality, and anyone who wants to consult them must make a pilgrimage to them. But now Asclepius was in a position to make epiphanies whenever he wished. From that time on this was the sole form of therapy which he practiced.[58] However, his original chthonic nature as a *genius loci* or local divinity remained evident, since his miraculous cures were only performed at his healing shrines, although he was now entitled to derive his mantic oracular character from his Olympian father Apollo.

From earliest times Apollo had been a god of oracles and healing. As a healer he is Apollo Maleatas, whose power of averting epidemics is described by Pausanias[59] and is compared with that of Pan Lyterius.[60] Aeschylus[61] calls Apollo *iatromantis* ("physician and seer"), and Aristophanes[62] *iatros kai mantis*. In magical therapy the combination of *praxis kai logos,* of treating with the hands and speaking (magic) words, is an essential feature (the German word for "to treat" is "be*hand*eln"). This may be why these two ideas are combined in Apollo.

We have already drawn attention to Apollo's ambivalent character as a god of healing. With his far-darting poisoned arrows he also sends plagues. Concerning these aspects of Apollo, *toxophoros* ("bow-bearing") and *apotoxeuōn* ("arrow-shooting"), the latter of which he is as *propylaios* ("standing before the gates"), consult G.F. Welcker's essay "Seuchen von Apol-

58 The miracles worked by Christian saints are also greater after their martyrdom than during their lifetime.

59 Pausanias ii. 32. 6.

60 Concerning Apollo as a god of healing, see R. Ganszyniec, *Arch. f. Gesch. d. Med.,* XV (1923), 33 ff.

61 Aeschylus *Eumenides* 62.

62 Aristophanes *Plutus* 11.

lon" (Plagues from Apollo).[63] The Christian God can even come dangerously close to Apollo as the god of pestilence, as may be seen from Gregor Erhart's Plague Monument at Rottweil (Plate 4).[64]

Soothsaying and the healing art are closely connected today not only in the case of holy miraculous cures but also wondrous medical cures. These cures will always be regarded as ambiguous and controversial. The reawakened controversy between doctors and "quacks" points up the need to investigate these cures from this point of view. The same applies to psychotherapy as a medical discipline, for many medical colleagues equate psychotherapy with charlatanism. It is not altogether surprising that they should do so. The psychotherapist understands Cicero[65] when he says of such cures: "Male coniecta, maleque interpretata, falsa sunt non rerum vitio, sed interpretum inscitia" ("badly surmised and badly interpreted, they are deceptive not because of their inherent falsity but because of the inexperience of those who interpret them").

Marvelous cures have a tendency to occur in particular places, for sanctity is bound up with locality. The new occupant of an oracle had to drive out his predecessor (*hērōs iatros,* "hero-physician"), but, despite the divine freedom of movement, the numen continued to be a ruling principle in its own sanctuary. Asclepius drove out Apollo Cyparissius[66] in Cos and Apollo Maleatas in Epidaurus. Nevertheless, the inscriptions recording cures at Epidaurus are still in piety called *Iamata tou Apollōnos kai tou Asklēpiou* ("healing miracles of Apollo and Asclepius"). Thus in antiquity countless healing shrines were firmly bound to

63 Welcker, *Kleine Schriften,* III, 33 ff. The "motive" of the missiles causing disease has lately been carefully studied by Lauri Honko in "Untersuchungen über eine urtümliche Krankheitserklärung," *Academia Scientiarum Fennica* (Helsinki, 1959), pp. 258 ff.

64 I am particularly grateful to Professor Julius Baum for drawing my attention to this monument.

65 Cicero *De divin.* i. 118.

66 Herzog, "Heilige Gesetze von Kos," p. 33.

Plate 4
Plague Memorial by Gregor Erhart in the Chapel of St. Laurence, Rottweil. To the right is a man sick with the plague, to the left the Madonna with a protective cloak which defends the faithful from God's plague-bearing arrows. My thanks are due to the late Professor Dr. Julius Baum of Stuttgart for supplying this photograph.

one geographical spot, just as they are today. Looked at psychologically, this means nothing less than a geography of the human psyche, which is further confirmed by the geographical particulars appearing in dreams. These facts explain the psychological "efficacy" of certain points on the surface of the planet.

The metamorphosis of Asclepius just described is essentially an *ascensus ad superos*. This change is psychologically interesting. The physician, through *intercessio divina,* leaves the earthly plane, rising to a higher one. Then the whole healing process takes place at a different and higher level. The god's retention of his chthonic qualities even as an Olympian figure is both surprising and extremely significant. And, too, he accomplishes his cures on the lower, earthly plane almost entirely by means of these chthonic qualities. Thus, despite the Olympian freedom which he now possesses, he remains true to the type of the chthonii, who are bound to their own locality. In this connection we quote an apt passage of the renowned Latin alchemical treatise *Tabula Smaragdina:* "Ascendit a terra in coelum, iterumque descendit in terram, et recipit vim superiorum et inferiorum" ("he ascends to Heaven from earth, and again descends to earth, and is endowed with the strength of the Powers above and below").

Asclepius thus unites not only man-and-god opposites but also chthonic and Olympian ones. His statue at Epidaurus shows him seated on a throne on which the dog and also Bellerophon with the Chimaera and Perseus with the head of Medusa are represented.[67] The connection with the Gorgon is explained by a passage from Apollodorus:[68]

> And after he had become a surgeon, bringing that art to great perfection, he not only saved men from death, but even raised them up from the dead. He had received from Athena blood from the veins of the Gorgon. He used the blood from the left side for plagues for mankind, and he

67 Pausanias ii. 27. 2.
68 Apollodorus *Bibl.* iii. 10. 3. 8-9.

> used that from the right for healing and to raise up men from the dead.

This is one of the few passages which show that Asclepius had a dark side. As a rule this dark side is seen only in his father Apollo. The motif of *ho trōsas iasetai* ("he who wounds also heals"), appearing here in the Gorgon's blood, which coming from one side slays and from the other conquers death, is so important from the psychological point of view that I quote also this passage from Tatian:[69]

> And after the Gorgon was beheaded ... Athena and Asclepius divided the drops of blood between them. And the latter received healing power. The former, however, became through that same shed blood a murderess of men [the instigatress of war].

It is noteworthy that while for Apollodorus the pair of opposites, light and dark, is still united in the symbol of Asclepius, for Tatian, with his hostility to things Greek, they have fallen apart.

In addition to the pair of opposites which has just been mentioned, Asclepius also unites within himself the opposites boy and man. He appears in a number of inscriptions as a *pais* ("boy"),[70] in contrast to the usual statue in which he is shown as a bearded man. In Megalopolis Asclepius had two sanctuaries, and in the second he was worshiped exclusively as a boy. His statue there is about three feet in height.[71] Asclepius was also worshiped in this form at Thelpusa.[72] The celebrated Boethus (second century B.C.) made a statue of Asclepius as a newborn child,[73] which the physician Nicomedes dedicated in the Roman temple of

69 Tatian *Adv. Graecos* 8. 2, 3.
70 *IG*, XIV, No. 976a and b.
71 Pausanias viii. 32. 4.
72 *Ibid.* viii. 25. 6.
73 P.-W., *s.v.* "Boethos."

Asclepius in the third century A.D. In dedicating this statue, Nicomedes[74] touches on the "mother-and-child" motif, probably not without a side glance at the Christian representations of the Madonna and child which were already current. The equation Asclepius-Pais equals Harpocrates is supported by the fact that to the Neo-Platonists Asclepius was the son of Apollo-Helios, just as Harpocrates was the son of Serapis-Helios. Asclepius appears as a handsome youth in some of the Epidaurian miraculous cures.[75] According to Deubner[76] the same theme is frequent in the dream apparitions of the Christian miraculous healers.

As a god of light, Asclepius united in himself a particularly striking pair of opposites, that of the sun and moon. Usener[77] has drawn attention to this, pointing out that Asclepius is often given the same epithets as Helios.[78] Pausanias[79] compares the course of the sun with the health of the human body. Eusebius[80] says in so many words: "If however Asclepius was to them also Helios, then ..."

Joannes Lydus[81] says that Isis was to the Egyptians the same as Asclepius to the Greeks, namely sun and health; whereas Macrobius[82] identifies Asclepius with the sun and Hygieia with the moon. The lunar quality of Asclepius himself emerges quite clearly from Hesychius:[83] "But the moon also is so called, even as Asclepius."

74 *IG*, XIV, No. 967a and b.
75 Herzog, *WHE*, Miracles XIV, XVI, XVII, XXXI.
76 L. Deubner, *De incubatione*, passim.
77 H. Usener, *Rhein. Mus.*, XLIX (1894).
78 Cf. C.F.H. Bruchmann and I.B. Carter in Roscher, *Lexikon*, Suppl. Certain epithets which are not mentioned by Bruchmann are given by Alice Walton, *The Cult of Asclepius*, Cornell Studies in Classical Philology No. 3 (New York, 1894), p. 35: *Aiglaēr* (Laconia), *Aglaopēs* (Hesych.), *aglaos*, which all have to do with radiance (Mionnet, *Desc. des médailles antiques grecques et romaines*, VI, 572, 70), and *aglaotimos* (*Orph. Hym.* 67. 6).
79 Pausanias vii. 23. 8.
80 εἰ δὲ καὶ Ἀσκληπιὸς πάλιν αὐτοῖς εἴη ὁ ἥλιος..., Eusebius *Praep. evang.* iii. 13, 19.
81 Joannes Lydus, *De mensibus* iv. 45.
82 Macrobius *Sat.* i. 21. 1.
83 ἀλλὰ καὶ ἡ σελήνη οὕτω καλεῖται καὶ ὁ Ἀσκληπιός, Hesychius, *s.v.* Αἴγλη.

Many other similar pairs of opposites could be mentioned. These are found united, however, not so much in Asclepius himself as in him and his family, as can be seen by Macrobius' statement above. To my mind the most important point here is that Asclepius can hardly be thought of without his feminine companions, his wife and daughters. There were Epione (the gentle one),[84] Hygieia, Panacea,[85] Iaso,[86] and others, each of whom was at times wife and at other times daughter. The fair maiden Hygieia seemed, to judge from sculptures, to have had a particularly good relation to the serpent of Asclepius, which she is shown feeding (Plate 5). She is addressed in the Orphic hymns[87] as *ēpiocheir Hygieia* ("Hygieia of the gentle hands"). This same quality of *malakai cheires* ("soft hands") is ascribed to Epione in the epigram of Crinagoras:[88]

> Hera, mother of the Ilithyiae, and thou, Hera, perfectress (*teleia*), and Zeus, the common father of all who are born, hear my prayer and grant that gentle pangs may come to Antonia in the tender hands of Hepione, so that her husband may rejoice and her mother and her mother-in-law. Her womb bears the blood of great houses.
>
> (translation by W.R. Paton)

From the epigram it is seen that the gentle, soft hands of Epione had an important therapeutic quality of special value for safe childbirth.

There were also men in the family of Asclepius, among them his son Machaon,[89] the slayer or wounder (*ho trōsas!*), and

84 Epione as wife of Asclepius: Cornutus *Theol. Graec. comp.* c. 33, and Scholiast on Lycophron *Alex.* 1054.

85 Scholiast on Aristophanes *Plut.* 701: Πανάκεια δὲ παρὰ τὸ ἄκος τὴν θεραπείαν ("Panakeia was named from the word 'akos' [remedy] of medical treatment.") Hence our word "panacea."

86 *Ibid.* 639 and 701, from ἰᾶσθαι = "to heal."

87 *Orphic Hymns* xxiii. 8 and xix. 18.

88 *Palatine Anthology* vi. 244.

89 *Iliad* xi. 516-17: "And with him went Machaon, son of Asclepius, the good leech."

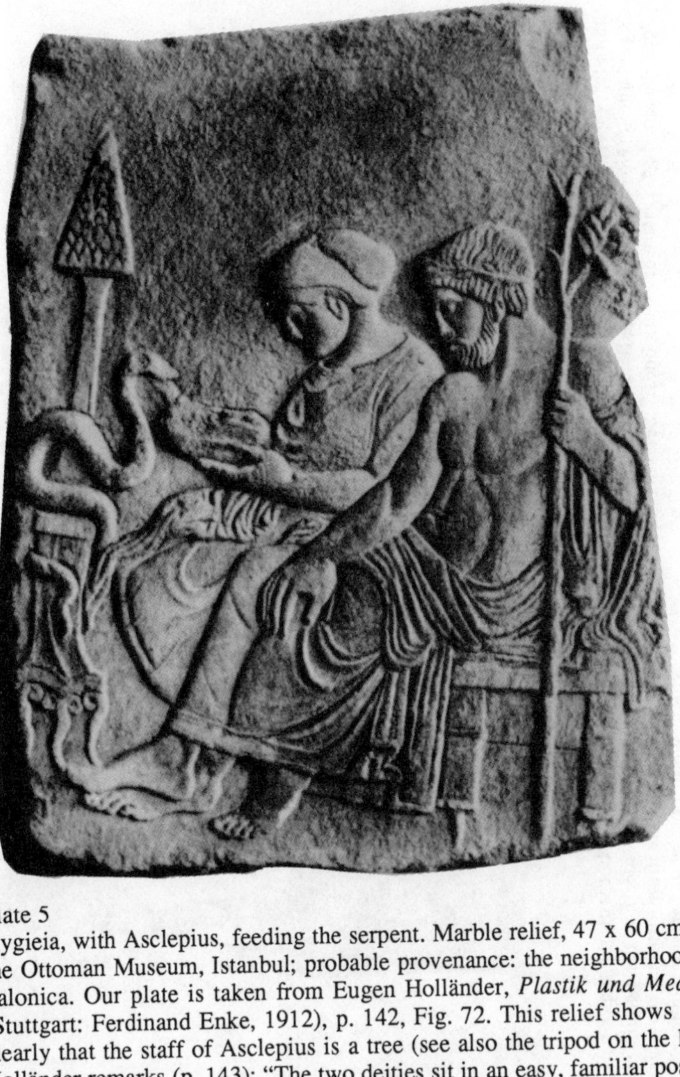

Plate 5
Hygieia, with Asclepius, feeding the serpent. Marble relief, 47 x 60 cm., in the Ottoman Museum, Istanbul; probable provenance: the neighborhood of Salonica. Our plate is taken from Eugen Holländer, *Plastik und Medizin* (Stuttgart: Ferdinand Enke, 1912), p. 142, Fig. 72. This relief shows very clearly that the staff of Asclepius is a tree (see also the tripod on the left). Holländer remarks (p. 143): "The two deities sit in an easy, familiar posture in front of a tripod around which the serpent has coiled itself. The god's robe has slipped down. It is not obvious at first glance to which of the two figures the three visible feet belong. Hygieia wears a garment with sleeves; the god is wearing a wreath and holds in his left hand the staff which he has just cut for himself; it still has a bunch of leaves on it. He looks on with interest as his companion feeds the snake."

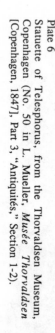

Plate 6
Statuette of Telesphorus, from the Thorvaldsen Museum, Copenhagen (No. 50 in L. Mueller, *Musée Thorvaldsen* [Copenhagen, 1847], Part 3, "Antiquités," Section 1-2).

Plate 7
The same statuette, but with the upper part removed and placed on the right-hand side. For the details see the text opposite. (Plates 6 and 7 are from original photographs 10.5 x 16 cm., which were obtained for the author by Dr. O. Brüel of Copenhagen with the kind permission of the Thorvaldsen Museum director, Mr. Sigurd Schultz.)

Podalirius.[90] The fact that the god had many children is important because fruitfulness and renewal (as in the case of the snake, cf. above) are closely connected with healing.[91] Another figure associated with Asclepius, especially in Pergamum, is that of Telesphorus,[92] the boy who fulfilled dreams and prayers.[93] Welcker[94] associates his name with *teletai;* this alludes to the connection with the mysteries. Telesphorus, too, is a *pais*.

Asclepius often appears in dreams with a whole *thiasos* of *paides* (band or group of boys). In Miracle LIX from Epidaurus[95] there are five, wearing cloaks.[96] This may be a foreshadowing of the modern practice of the chief doctor, accompanied by his students, making his rounds.

Telesphorus is entirely muffled up in his curious *bardocucullus* (hooded overcoat) and looks like the "Münchner Kindl." In inscriptions he is often characterized with Asclepius and Hygieia as *theoi sōtēres,* or alone as *sōtēr*.[97] He is *zōophoros* and *pyrphoros* ("life-bringing" or "fire-bearing"). He sends true dreams, *oneirata telesphora*.[98] In the Thorvaldsen Museum in Copenhagen there is a statuette of Telesphorus with a removable top concealing a phallus (Plates 6 and 7). It was donated to the collection by Thorvaldsen in 1838, but its origin is unknown. Mueller[99] describes it as follows:

> "No. 50. Walking Telesphorus with arms wrapped in a short coat that covers the back of the head and rises to a high point; around its loins it wears a cloth and also has

90 *Iliad* ii. 731-32: "Of these again Asclepius' two sons were leaders, the cunning leeches Podalirius and Machaon."

91 Cf. p. 20.

92 Τελεσφόρος Ἀσκληπιοῦ, *IG,* III^1, No. 1159, and together with Hygieia and Asclepius, as θεοὶ σωτῆρες (savior-gods).

93 H. Usener, *Götternamen* (2nd ed.; Bonn, 1929), p. 171.

94 F.G. Welcker, *Götterlehre* (1857-62), II, 740.

95 Herzog, *WHE*.

96 χλανδηφόρων πέντε

97 *IG,* IV, No. 1044, from Epidaurus; cf. n. 92, above.

98 Friedrich Schwenn in P.-W., *s.v.* "Telesphorus."

99 Mueller, Musée Thorvaldsen. Troisième Partie, Antiquités, Sections 1-2, Copenhague 1847, p. 162 f.

shoes on. At the same time the upper part of the body is represented in the form of a phallus (like a priapic demon – Tychon, or Fascinus, or Mutunus) in that the top of the figure is hollow and can be lifted off to reveal an ithyphallus that is a continuation of the lower part."

The statuette is of bronze, and its lower part is 7.2 cm high, while the upper part is 6.9 cm. The overall height is 10.5 cm. I would like to thank Sigurd Schultz, the Director of the Thorvaldsen Museum, both for providing this information and for allowing us to publish photographs of the piece for the first time (Plates 6 and 7). According to Panofka[100] the statuette bears the inscription *Omorion*. But Mr. Sigurd Schultz[101] states that it "bears no trace of an inscription at all." Panofka translates *Omorion* by the rather strange term "boundary neighbor." Ithyphallic, hermlike boundary stones are of course well known, but they refer quite definitely to Hermes and are as a rule very much larger. Panofka's interpretation is all the more difficult to understand because he refers to an earlier publication of his on a marble sculpture of Tychon,[102] where he describes a similar figure in marble relief and quotes the following passage from Photius:[103]

> But I, who have had this nuptial chamber built, will address my prayers to the goddess Tyche and to the Loves, the givers of fruitfulness, who cause the generation of legitimate children, so that through the marriage cakes we too may enter into union for the generation of children.

100 Th. Panofka, "Asklepios und die Asklepiaden," *Abhandl. der Königl. Akademie der Wiss. zu Berlin, 1845* (Berlin 1847), pp. 271-359.
101 Letter to the author.
102 Th. Panofka, in Gerhard's *Archäologische Zeitung*, II, No. 15 (1844), 249.
103 Photius *Bibl.* (ed. Bekker, Vol. II, p. 367) (1113 R).

It has been emphasized by Weinreich and others that the equation chthonic = phallic = *alexikakos* ("averter of evil") is valid. In any case, as may be seen from Petronius,[104] Priapus, too, is a god of healing.

A similar ithyphallic dwarf, Harpocrates, is as indispensable to Serapis, the Alexandrian god of healing, as Telesphorus is to Asclepius. These dwarfs present a great similarity to the Idaean Dactyls and the Cabiri. Telesphorus, moreover, was first worshiped in Pergamum, where the cult of the Cabiri was very ancient. At Pergamum he is characterized in inscriptions as *zōophoros,* "life-bringing, generating," and as *phaësimbrotos,* "bringing light to mortal men." A large number of votive tablets show such a boy standing beside the god at a sickbed.[105] The boy's clothing is reminiscent of the ancient statue of Asclepius at Titane.[106] Both have the same doll-like expression and are so completely muffled up that nothing can be seen except the face, feet and fingers. It is also worth noting that Asclepius was identified in Phoenicia with the indigenous gods there (Esmun), and thus made into a brother of the Cabiri.[107]

Rhea's fingers were caught in the maternal earth of Mount Ida.[108] Her fingers became the Idaean Dactyls, who possessed generative power. Therefore they were accounted gods of healing embodying creative power in the touch. The reader will remember the gesture of the outstretched hand in the picture of the creation of Adam in Michelangelo's frescoes in the Sistine Chapel. When Zeus healed Io of her madness by stretching out his hand over her (*epaphōn kai thigōn,* "laying on hands and touching"), she gave birth, although a virgin, to Epaphus. From this Zeus derived the epithet Zeus Epaphus, "he who

104 Petronius 133 *Priapeum* XXXVII. Cf. H. Herter, "De Priapo," *RGVV,* XXIII (1932), 233.

105 Cf. Suidas *Lexikon, s.v.* θεόπομπος.

106 Pausanias ii. 11. 6.

107 *Ibid.* vii. 23. 8; Damascius *Vita Isidori* 302.

108 Anonymus Ambr. *De re metr.* in Studemund *Varia,* I, 224, pars. 6, 27 ff.; Nonnos *Dionysiaca* xiv. 23 ff.

touches."[109] In connection with Zeus Epaphus, Maas shows that Dionysus Epaphius is identical with Dionysus Lysius.[110] Apollo as a healing god also uses the gesture of stretching out his hand over the sick person. From this he receives the epithet Apollo *hyperdexios* ("holding his hand over"). Healing by a touch of the hand is also implied in the names of Chiron and Dexion (an Attic healing hero worshiped with Amynus – a still older healing hero – and later with Asclepius and Dexione[111]). The names Zeus Hyperdexius, Athene Hyperdexia, Apollo Hyperdexius, Hera Hyperchiria and Persephone Chirogonia speak the same language.[112] Chiron as *cheirourgos* ("working by hand, practicing a handcraft or art"; *Chirurg* = German for "surgeon") has degenerated into chiropractor in our day. The idea that the finger possesses generative power no doubt underlies the German expression "to suck something out of one's fingers," meaning to invent or supply something.

The part played by the finger in healing charms is well known. Alexander of Tralles[113] writes of the *iatrikos daktylos* (medical finger) and Pliny[114] of the *digitus medicus*. Macrobius[115] and Bachofen[116] deal with the *digitus medicinalis* of the statues of gods, which was anointed. It is noteworthy that in Greek *cheires* (hands) and *dynameis* ([divine] powers) are equated,[117] and that in Latin the word *manus* means both the hand and a body of troops. Further, kings and emperors –

109 Aeschylus *Prometheus Bound* 848-51:

> There Zeus shall calm thy madness by his hand
> Casting out fear, whose touch is all in all
> Therefrom shall spring a child, whom men shall call,
> In memory of the magic of that Hand,
> Dark Epaphus. (trans. Gilbert Murray)

110 Maas, *De Aeschyli Supplicibus*, Index lectionum (Gryphiswald, 1890-1891), p. 16.

111 Cf. F. Kutsch, "Attische Heilgötter und Heilheroen," *RGVV*, XII, 3.

112 O. Weinreich, *AHW*, p. 18, n. 5.

113 Alexander of Tralles ii. 199 (ed. Puschmann).

114 Pliny *Hist nat.* xxx. 108.

115 Macrobius *Sat.* vii. 13. 9.

116 J.J. Bachofen, *Mutterrecht* (Basel, 1948), pp. 130 a, b and 131 a.

117 Cf. Ch. A. Lobeck, *Aglaophamus* (Königsberg, 1829), pp. 885 f. and 951.

Pyrrhus, Vespasian and Hadrian are examples – used to heal disease by the laying-on of hands, a practice continued until after the end of the Middle Ages by the English and French kings, especially for the "king's evil [epilepsy]." The gesture has been preserved up to the present day in ecclesiastical ritual.

For Io the act of healing resulted in *generation,* and was thus clearly *gennēma* ("conception"), leading to virginal conception. It is significant in this connection that the soothsayer Melampus, who healed by means of incantations,[118] inaugurated the Phallophoria[119] after he had healed the daughters of Proetus of Dionysiac madness. If O. Wolff is correct, then the Melampodeum was a circular structure out of which there grew a tree with a serpent coiled round it.[120]

118 Ovid *Metamorphoses* xv. 326-59.

119 Herodotus ii. 49.

120 O. Wolff in Roscher, *Lexikon,* II, 2572. Cf. also pp. 64-66, below, and Weinreich, *AHW,* Ch. I, ΘΕΟΥ–ΧΕΙΡ, for other examples.

Plate 8
Serapis statuette.
Bronze, 16.4 cm. high, Alexandrian, Vienna, private collection.

CHAPTER IV

SERAPIS

THE ALEXANDRIAN DEITY SERAPIS was the only other ancient healing god besides Asclepius to survive the advent of Christianity by about four hundred years. The Serapis cult was introduced[1] into Alexandria by the first Ptolemy, Ptolemaeus Soter, in the last decades of the fourth century B.C. after consultation of the Delphic oracle.[2] Alexander the Great was also a devotee of Serapis. He dedicated his spear and breastplate to him at Gortys[3] and instituted festivals for him at Soli.[4] Shortly before his death, Alexander successfully consulted Serapis by means of incubation in the land of Babylon.[5]

The translation of a colossal statue of Serapis to Egypt from Sinope on the Black Sea was carried out on instructions given in a dream. Typically, a chthonic deity, Darzales, accompanied by a female companion, has been excavated at the latter site.[6] Tacitus describes Serapis as a supernaturally beautiful *youth* – note the recurrence of the idea of the *pais*. The image and cult of Serapis were subsequently developed in Egypt in a typically syncretistic way with the assistance of the Egyptian high priest, Manetho of Sebennytus, and the Greek exegete and Eumolpid of Eleusis, Timotheus. Clearly it is no accident that an Eleusinian mystagogue played a decisive part in this matter.[7] Serapis was represented bearing the *modius* ("cornucopia"), with golden rays,

1 For full details about the introduction of this cult, cf. Tacitus *Histories* iv. 83 ff.

2 Plutarch *De Iside et Osiride* and *De sollert. animae* xxxvi. Cf. E. Schmidt, "Kultübertragungen," *RGVV*, VIII, 2, 3.

3 Pausanias viii. 28. 1.

4 Arrian *Anabasis* ii. 5. 8 and O. Weinreich, *Neue Urkunden zur Sarapisreligion* (Tübingen, 1919). For Alexander's connection with Epidaurus, cf. Arrian *Anabasis* vii. 14. 5, 6.

5 Arrian *Anabasis* vii. 26. 2.

6 O. Weinreich, *op. cit.*

7 Cf. p. 108.

representing the sun. These represent the opposites of earth and heaven, which have already been noted in connection with Asclepius. In syncretistic Alexandria, Serapis was known in the Egyptian tongue as Osiris-Apis, that is, Usur- or Usar-Apî, whence his name Sar-Apis; thus he was conceived as ruler of the dead and as an earth god. In the Greek language he was known as Hades, or, as Plutarch[8] relates, as Asclepius, because his image, like that of Asclepius, bore the *kerberos kai drakōn* (Cerberus and snake), dog and serpent. This statement is confirmed by the sculptures which have been preserved. Furthermore, the serpent is always represented as coiled round a tree stump or staff, just as it is in the statues of Asclepius. For this reason, according to Tacitus,[9] many identified him with Asclepius, and Aristides saw him in a vision in a form exactly identical with that of Asclepius. Thus it is not surprising that Serapis made his way into Greece and Rome, where, as Aristides[10] relates, he had forty-two temples. His most famous sanctuaries were the ones at Canopus, described by Strabo,[11] and the one at Alexandria, which survived until A.D. 391, when it was destroyed by order of the fanatical Bishop Theophilus. Unfortunately, authentic records of miraculous cures are lost, but a few have been reported by Artemidorus.[12] Aristides[13] calls Serapis *philanthrōpotatos* ("who loves man most" or "most benevolent toward mankind").

As has been stated, Serapis was accompanied by a dwarf, Harpocrates, just as Asclepius was by Telesphorus. According to Plutarch, Harpocrates is the posthumous weakly son of Isis and Osiris and is thus the typical divine child. He, too, is depicted with gigantic genitals, carrying a cornucopia – that is, his generative aspect is strongly emphasized. Another characteristic point is that he holds his finger to his lips. This may be an

8 Plutarch *De Iside et Osiride* 28.
9 Tacitus *Histories* iv. 84. 5.
10 Aristides 500. 19 (ed. Dindorf).
11 Strabo xvii. 1, 17.
12 Artemidorus *Oneirocr.* ii. 44.
13 Aristides ii, p. 360 (par. 26 K).

allusion to the command to keep silent concerning the mysteries (*daktylos katasigazōn,* "silent finger"). The idea of *favere linguis,* "keep guard over the tongue," which is related to that of *euphēmein,* "to keep a religious silence," has an importance in psychotherapeutic practice which should not be underestimated.

Serapis was as a matter of fact always *synnaos* ("in the same sanctuary"), that is, "sharing a temple," with Isis, just as Asclepius did with Hygieia,[14] and he, too, is not to be thought of without his feminine companion. In a large number of sculptures *she* is accompanied by the dog, which is then Sirius (Isis-Sothis). Sirius, the hound of the hunter Orion,[15] which was placed among the stars, was personified at quite an early date in Egypt as the goddess Sothis. Later this goddess was identified with Isis, because the dog days bring the overflowing of the Nile – the tears of Isis – and so fertilize the land. Anubis, the dog-headed god, likewise was identified with Sirius.[16] Isis had always healed disease.[17] In her most famous temple at Menuthis near Canopus, she did not cease to work cures until Bishop Cyrillus moved the bones of the Christian martyrs Cyrus and John there, whereupon their miraculous cures outdid hers. Yet her healing activity is much older. She cured her son Horus and taught him the art of healing. Welcker believes that she did not begin to practice medicine until she was associated with Serapis. Diodorus,[18] however, places the beginning of her medical activities much earlier, and the Papyrus Ebers (1700 B.C.) bears him out, for there she is said to have prepared a remedy for Ra to rid him of his headache. Her cult was introduced into Athens and Corinth (at Cenchrae, the port of Corinth) in the fourth century B.C.; but she did not begin her public healing activity there until she had become associated with Serapis.

14 Isis with Asclepius: Pausanias vii. 26. 7 (Aegira) and ii. 2. 3 (Cenchrae); with Asclepius and Serapis: Pausanias iii. 23. 23 (Boeae).

15 Hesiod *Erga* 417 and 609.

16 Cf. pp. 20.

17 Cf. Joannes Lydus, *De mens*. iv. For reports of cures see Roscher, *Lexikon*, II, 524.

18 Diodorus i. 25.

The serpent-wreathed staff is to be seen on the altar of Isis at Pola as well as on a tessera in the Museo Numismatico C. Filippo Lavy (tessera I.407 4582 R). In the temple of Isis at Pompeii there are two serpents at the extreme left of the altar, each coiled around a staff.[19] The goddess is often shown in Greco-Roman sculptures riding on a dog, and she is often accompanied by the dwarf Harpocrates. At Memphis Asclepius was identified with Osiris and thus became the husband of Isis, according to Tacitus.[20]

The far-reaching connection between Asclepius and Serapis is also shown by the very numerous acclamations and inscriptions on Serapis-*telesmata* (talismans): *Zeus Hēlios Sarapis* or "Zeus-Serapis is One," just as Asclepius was often called simply *Zeus Asklēpios*.[21] Asclepius and Serapis, as well as many other chthonic demons, derive the designation "Zeus" from *Zeus katachthonios* (Zeus of the Underworld). In this connection it is also necessary to bear in mind Zeus Meilichius, who always had a great serpent as his attribute.[22] Zeus with a chthonic *synnaos* or *symbōmos* ("same altar" – that is, with a chthonic being sharing his temple or altar) is described by Wide.[23] As regards the dark side of his wife Hera, as Catachthonia, it need only be recalled that she gave birth to Typhon, nourished the Lernaean Hydra, sent the serpents to Hercules, and struck Io, Hercules, Dionysus, the Proetides, Athamas and Ino with madness.

The practice of healing at the sanctuaries of Serapis was largely the same as at the sanctuaries of Asclepius. This is described in the next chapter. As Plate 9 shows, in Ptolemaic Egypt there were also Greek dream interpreters working near the sanctuaries of Serapis.

19 For further material on the connection between Isis and the sacred serpent, cf. W. Drexler in Roscher, *Lexikon*, II, 533-39.

20 Tacitus *Histories* iv. 84.

21 Cf. Aristides *Oratio* L. 46 and A.B. Cook, *Zeus* (1925), II, Pt. 2, 1076 ff.

22 Cf. J.E. Harrison, *Prolegomena to the Study of Greek Religion* (2nd ed.; Cambridge, 1908), pp. 18 ff., Plates 1 and 2 : Reliefs from the Piraeus (Berlin. Mus. Kat. Nos. 722 and 723).

23 Sam Wide, "Chthonische und himmlische Götter," *Arch. Rel. Wiss.*, X (1907), 257-68.

Plate 9

Sign of an Egyptian dream interpreter in the Ptolemaic era in Memphis (Gizeh Museum), treated by Otto Rubensohn. The text runs: "I interpret dreams on behalf of the deity. Beloved be Tyche! This is a Cretan who interprets such things here."

Below is the Serapis bull, indicating that dream interpreters are working near the Serapis temple at Memphis.

CHAPTER V

INCUBATION RITUAL IN THE SANCTUARIES OF ASCLEPIUS

We are such stuff
As dreams are made on; and our little life
is rounded with a sleep.
Shakespeare, *Tempest* IV. i

EARLIER I MENTIONED that very little reliable information is available about the rites practiced in the sanctuaries of Asclepius. We know for certain that from near and far there came to the *hieron* (the sanctuary), which was generally situated in a very remote spot, sick people who hoped to be cured – especially if medical skill had proved unavailing or held out no hope. In this respect therapeutic optimism was unbounded and was never disappointed;[1] for Asclepius was the "true and competent physician," as Aristides[2] calls him. If, however, the patients were on the point of death or if they were women near to childbirth, they were ordered to remain outside the sanctuary,[3] for this had to be kept ritually clean.[4] A similar rule of ritual purity applied to the island of Delos.[5] This "cruel" rule was of course grist to the mill of envious rivals of the cult of Asclepius, the doctors of the ancient world and, later, the Fathers of the Church. Yet even St. Thecla, who was famous for her miraculous cures, did not permit anyone to be buried in her church in Seleucia.[6]

1 Cf. O. Weinreich, *AHW*, Appendix I.
2 τὸν ἀληθινὸν καὶ προσήκοντα ἡμῖν ἰατρόν, Aristides ii, p. 389 (par. 57, ed. Keil).
3 Pausanias ii. 27. 1 and 6.
4 Cf. Eugen Fehrle, "Die kultische Keuschheit im Altertum," *RGVV*, VI (1910).
5 The same rule applied to the precinct on the Lycaeum in Arcadia which was sacred to Zeus, according to K. Kerényi.
6 L. Deubner, *De Incubatione* (Leipzig, 1900); cf. also Theodor Wächter, "Reinheitsvorschriften im griechischen Kult," *RGVV*, IX, Pt. 1 (1910), 25 ff. and 43 ff.

In Japanese Shintoism the practice of sleeping within the temple precincts is also known. So far as we can tell, the ritual is exactly the same; for example, the sacred precinct on the island of Itsuku-shima must be kept unpolluted by birth or death, and sacred animals are also kept in the sanctuary.[7]

Before the actual rite of incubation took place, certain rites of purification and ablutions had to be performed. Porphyrius[8] reports an inscription in Epidaurus which runs:

> Let every man who enters the incense-laden temple be clean,
> Yet he may be called clean who has none but holy thoughts
> in his mind.

An inscription in the Asclepieium at Lambaesis in Africa runs:

> *Bonus intra, melior exi* [9]
> ("Go in good, come out better.")

An initial cleansing bath seems to have been one of the necessary preliminaries for incubation. In the ancient world the bath was thought of as having a purifying effect on the soul as well as the body,[10] since it freed the soul from contamination by the body and thus set the soul free for communion with the god. The *mystai* (participants in the Mysteries at Eleusis) were also required to bathe.[11]

After the preliminary sacrifices had been made, the sick person slept in the *abaton* or *adyton* (*abaton* = "inmost sanctuary"). The god of sleep, Hypnos Epidotes (the generous) and the god of dreams, Oneiros, had statues in the Asclepieium at Sicyon,[12] and an Attic inscription names Asclepius, Hygieia and Hypnos

7 Emil Schiller, *Shinto, die Volksreligion Japans* (1911).
8 Porphyrius *De abstinentia* ii. 19.
9 *CIL*, VIII, 2584.
10 Cf. Plato *Cratylus* 405 B.
11 O. Kern, *Religion*, II, 198.
12 Pausanias ii. 13. 3.

together.[13] At Epidaurus, too, there are many dedicatory inscriptions to Hypnos.[14] It is of special interest that Asclepius himself is represented sleeping, that is, incubating:[15]

> Awake, Paieon Asclepius, commander of peoples,
> Gentle-minded offspring of Apollo and noble Coronis,
> Wipe the sleep from thine eyes and hear the prayer
> Of thy worshipers, who often and never in vain
> Try to incline thy power favorably, first through Hygieia.
> O gentle-minded Asclepius,
> Awake and hear thy hymn; greetings, thou bringer of weal!

Another person could sleep in the sanctuary as proxy for a sick person who could not be moved.[16] The problem was thus transferred to the representative, so that he could have dreams which were valid for the patient. The phenomenon of vicarious dreaming is not completely unknown in analysis.

When the sick slept in the abaton, they lay on a *klinē* ("couch"). Our modern clinics are proud to derive their name from this word. Yet, I am unaware of any clinic whose personnel remember that patients once lay on the couch to have healing dreams. Often the *klinē* stood near the *agalma* (the god's statue or statue in honor of the god) in the temple as, for instance, in the Asclepian sanctuary at Tithorea.[17] Not until some two thousand years later did doctors with a psychological outlook, following Freud's example, again use the couch. More recent developments in the direction of the dialectical method of C.G. Jung have, however, led to the abandonment of the analytical couch, and instead, doctor and patient sit face to face on the same level. The *klinē* appears symbolically as constellating the unconscious in the following contemporary dream:

13 W. Dittenberger, *Sylloge* 2, II, No. 776.
14 *IG,* IV, Nos. 1048, 1335 and 1336.
15 G. Kaibel, *Epigrammata Graeca* (Berlin, 1878), Epigram No. 1027, p. 433.
16 Cf. Strabo xvii, p. 801; Herodotus viii. 134; Pausanias x. 38. 13; and Deubner, *op. cit.*, p. 85.
17 Pausanias x. 32. 12.

IV. I am lying on a couch; on my right, near my head, there is a precious stone, perhaps set in a ring, which has the power to make every image that I want to see visible in a living form. . . .

The relation of the modern dreamer to the precious stone, as a more or less abstract symbol of the self, corresponds to that of the ancient incubant to Asclepius. The precious stone also fulfills the function of the crystal ball in prophecy, that is, it serves as a "yantra" (charm) for the visualization of unconscious contents.

Abaton or *adyton* means "place not to be entered unbidden." Here we must conjecture about the rite and assume that those permitted to sleep in the temple were those bidden or called to do so. For sick persons healed on Tiber Island, the invariable formula used was *echrēmatisen ho theos* ("the god made it be known by means of an oracle that he would appear"). According to Pausanias,[18] the greatest sanctuary of Isis in Greece, Tithorea, could be entered only by those the goddess had invited in a dream. The same practice was followed by the so-called Catachthonioi, who also descended into the earth, as their name shows, in the cities on the Maeander. Philostratus[19] relates that the sick did not go to Apollonius of Tyana except at the behest of Asclepius. Probably being bidden by the god was the original significance of incubation. It is, at the same time, the first allusion to the mystery character of the cult of Asclepius.

We know that the goddess Isis invited those she wished to come to the temple for her mysteries by means of a dream. But she punished those who came uninvited.[20] Apuleius knew that he must be summoned by the goddess, otherwise he would die if he entered the *adyton*. We do not know whether a summons was sent to the suppliants of Asclepius.[21] It was decisive that the sick

18 *Ibid.* x. 32. 13.
19 Philostratus *Vita Ap. Tyan.* iv. 1 and 9; cf. Tacitus *Histories* iv. 81; Dio Cassius xxxxiv. 8.
20 Pausanias x. 12. 19.
21 Cf. pp. 107 ff.

should have the *right dream* while sleeping in the abaton. This was the essential point for the rite of incubation. The word *incubare* is aptly translated by Herzog[22] as "to sleep in the sacred precinct." This corresponds to the Greek phrase *enkoimasthai en tǭ abatǭ*. Pausanias sometimes calls the abaton simply *enkoimētērion* ("the sleeping-place"). The right dream brought the patient an immediate cure.[23] The two famous physicians Galen and Rufus[24] attest to this fact unreservedly. Apparently the incubant was always cured if Asclepius appeared in the dream.[25]

The god might appear *onar,* "in a dream," as the technical term was, or, alternatively *hypar,*[26] "in the waking state," or, as we should say, in a vision. He appeared in a form resembling his statue, that is, as a bearded man or a boy, or quite often in one of his theriomorphic forms, as a serpent[27] or a dog.[28] Generally he was accompanied by his female companions and sons. He himself, or, even more often, his serpent or dog, *touched* the affected part of the incubant's body[29] and then vanished. Welcker[30] quotes the following remark of Kieser's,[31] which is of great interest today: "Thus in cases where the inner sense of sickness is personified and expresses itself through symbols, a cure can take place."

22 Herzog, *WHE,* p. 5.

23 The equation dream = healing is apparent from Iamblichus *De mysteriis* 3. 3.

24 Galen *De libr. propr.* c. 2; Rufus in Oribasius *Collect. medicae* xxxxv. 30. 14.

25 Cf. *IG,* IV², 1, No. 127.

26 εἶδον καὶ τὸν Ἀσκληπιόν ἀλλ' οὐχὶ ὄναρ, "And I saw Asclepius, too, and not in a dream," Maximus Tyrius *Philosophoumena* ix. 7. i. Cf. also *Oxyrhynchus Papyrus* XI. 1381 (Praise of Ptah-Imuthes-Asclepius), where Column V, 108/9 contains an interesting contribution to the phenomenon of the σὺμπτωμα. For further remarks on this point, see p. 55 f.

27 For example, in the Epidaurian Iamata XVII, XXXIII, XXXIX, XLII, XLIV, XLV and LVII (numbering according to Herzog, *WHE*), and in Aristophanes *Plutus* 727 ff., and also on a dedicatory relief of Amphiaraon of Oropus, ed. Herzog, *WHE.*

28 For example, in Miracles XX and XVI, Herzog, *WHE.*

29 Cf. pp. 39-40.

30 F.G. Welcker, *Kleine Schriften* (Bonn, 1850), III, 7.

31 Kieser, in *Arch. f.d. tierischen Magnetismus,* by C.A. Eschenmeyer, Kieser and Nasse, II, 3, 126.

Originally, in all probability, the patient was thought incurable if he did not experience a dream or apparition on the first night. I regard this *ex iuvantibus* as confirmation of the hypothesis that it was necessary to be summoned to the healing mysteries of Asclepius. In any case, this emerges clearly from the Apellas stele[32] as well as from Miracle XLVIII.[33] The proposition then would run: "Only he is helped who is called." It is possible, however, that auguries and auspices were taken at the preliminary sacrifices and that the sick person did not sleep in the abaton unless these were favorable. This was certainly the case at a later date, since there is evidence that sick persons sometimes stayed for a considerable time at the Asclepieium. In such cases preliminary sacrifices were continued until a favorable constellation occurred, a *numen* of the deity which showed that the *kairos oxys* ("the decisive moment") had arrived. In Miracle IV,[34] Ambrosia of Athens, who is one-eyed, laughs at the idea that the halt and the blind should be cured after only one dream.[35]

An impressive example of this from the sixteenth century is to be found in Montaigne, in his "Journal de Voyage en Italie" IV (1581), where he gives an account of an incubation dream and healing experience that he had in Loreto. The following dream may be taken to represent similar experiences in modern times:

V. It was snowing and snowing until the snow was one meter deep, but still it wasn't winter. I want to go out and get my car, which is almost buried beneath the snow. But there is almost as much snow in the car itself. As I'm getting the snow out I notice that it is extremely light, like whisked egg-white. While this is going on, a stranger comes up to me on a toboggan and asks me to join him on the toboggan instead of using the car. I accept and he helps me onto the toboggan with the utmost care and tenderness.

32 Herzog, *WHE*, pp. 43-44.
33 Herzog, *WHE*. Cf. also Weinreich, *AHW*, p. 112.
34 Herzog, *WHE*.
35 ὑγιεῖς γίνεσθαι ἐνύπνιον ἰδόντας μόνον.

We go down the slope without speaking, but I am very aware of his presence behind me. When we get to the bottom, he tells me that it would be a good idea for me to go to a certain place and stay there. I obey and recognize the place as a sort of convalescent home. I can see a large room with odd sorts of frames (difficult to describe), but they are not beds. There are two or three people lying there, tied down with broad, white bandages. One of these frames is empty but the bandages are lying on it.

I am told that I must stay here for at least two to three months, completely immobile, that we are all suffering from the same illness and that this is the best remedy. I hesitated, thinking that there must be a different treatment. But I gave the matter careful thought and found that I was not worried at the prospect of staying here so long – let's do it, it might be worthwhile. But I was fully aware of the fact that despite the strong impression made upon me by the stranger and what he said, the decision rested solely with me. I agreed ... Then I heard a voice from far away saying that this was the only remedy; actually we had not realized at the beginning that we would otherwise have been incurable.

As regards the above, one should compare it with the remarks on page 92-93 concerning the *katochoi* (restrained) and the *desmioi* (chained).

It seems desirable to correct certain widely accepted assumptions about the practice of incubation in the Asclepieia in the early period. Dream interpreters did not practice in the sanctuaries. As we have seen, they were not necessary. Therefore it is also unlikely that the priests interpreted dreams. Similarly, there were no doctors in the sacred precincts, and medicine was not practiced there. The numerous priests were more probably therapeutae, in the sense of Galen's usage of the term.[36] This is also

36 Cf. p. 1.

shown by this passage from Aristides:[37] "All those round the god are therapeutae." In Athens, to cite one instance, priests were chosen by lot, so that there was no question of medical qualifications. Besides, it is not very likely that many of the patients would have survived if the surgical operations which played such a large part in their dreams had been taken literally.

Everyone cured was obliged to record his dream or to have it recorded – a requirement which we make of our patients today. The incubants were often given this command in the dream itself (*kat' onar),* and the inscribed records on the votive tablets were called *charistēria* ("thank offerings").[38] A similar instruction is to be found on the Apellas stele.

Apparently the patient had no further obligation after recording the dream, apart from certain thank offerings and the payment of the fee. People gave what they could, in proportion to their wealth.[39] But the thank offering which Asclepius preferred was a cock.[40] The fact that the dying Socrates remembered Asclepius shows that the ancient divine physician was helpful to the dying also; he could cure men of "the fever called living" (cf. *Macbeth* III. ii. 22-23: "Duncan is in his grave; After life's fitful fever he sleeps well…"). An Orphic hymn to Asclepius confirms this:

> Come, blessed one, helper, give to life a noble ending.[41]

An interesting light is thrown on Asclepius by the fact that the cock was also sacrificed to Hermes, Helios and Cora.

The thank offerings, called *iatra* or *sōstra,* could be paid at any time within a year. Cases are on record, however, where the god gave those who were too slow in paying their debts a sharp

37 πάντες οἱ περὶ τὸν θεὸν θεραπευταί, Aristides 477. 15 (ed. Dindorf).

38 Dittenberger, *Sylloge* II ^{2}, Nos. 805, 806,10 f.

39 Cf. Hesiod *Erga* 336: "And according to your powers make sacrifice to the eternal gods, in holiness and purity and with fine burnt offerings."

40 Plato *Phaedo* 118 A; Herondas *Mimiambus* iv. 11-13 (ed. Crusius-Herzog; Leipzig, 1926); and Aelian, Frags. 98^1 and 101^1.

41 ἰλθέ, μάκαρ, σωτὴρ βιοτῆς τέλος ἐσθλὸν ὀπάζων.

lesson by promptly sending a relapse. This was of course a great cause of scandal to the Early Fathers, who pointed out that Christian martyrs such as Cosmas and Damian, Cyrus and John, worked their miraculous cures as *anargyroi,* that is, free of charge. It appears to have escaped their notice, however, that the Christian thaumaturges, too, followed their predecessors very closely. Examples are to be found in Deubner.[42] The instances from Switzerland are probably not so well known; Ernst Baumann[43] quotes some interesting passages from Brother Klaus on this point.

It is thus not so very surprising that the ancients reabsorbed Cosmas and Damian into paganism as Castor and Pollux. This was all the more natural as both pairs appear as stars and as horses.[44] In Rome the church of Saints Cosmas and Damian is on the site of the ancient temple of the Dioscuri, who were worshiped there as healing gods. The same is true at Byzantium, where the site is also near a sanctuary of Amphiaraus. The motif of healing twins has already come up in connection with Asclepius' sons Machaon and Podalirius, one of whom, Machaon, is as usual mortal, while the other is immortal. These examples bring to mind the images of body and soul, both of which, as has been pointed out, were provided for in the ancient art of healing. I doubt, however, that this is the complete meaning of the theme. Experience in analytical psychology shows that the appearance of a pair of identical figures, which we call a "doublet," is as a rule associated with the emergence of material into consciousness. Emergence into consciousness, however, is closely related to healing. An almost literal example of the doublet motif is provided in the following dream episode:

VI. An unknown woman brings me some prunes as a dessert and at the same time a male voice in the background says:

42 Deubner, *op. cit.,* passim.
43 Ernst Baumann, "Volkskundliches zur Bruder Klausen Verehrung," *Schweiz. Arch. f. Volkskunde,* XLIII (1946), 296, n. 1.
44 Deubner, *op. cit.,* pp. 77 f.

> "You must eat this fruit in order to be able to make the experiment with the Zeeman effect...."[45]

Machaon and Podalirius naturally remind us of pairs of Christian saints, Cosmas and Damian, Cyrus and John. Aristides refers to the sons of Asclepius literally as the Dioscuri:[46]

> *ō Dioskourois isomoiroi kai hēlikiōtai en heterǭ chronǭ tēs geneseōs....*
>
> O ye whose destiny is like unto that of the Dioscuri, and are of the same age as they, albeit in another period of time....

Preller[47] calls Machaon the surgeon and Podalirius the practitioner of internal medicine, thus introducing an interesting typological contrast.

At this point I should like to mention two accounts of the sacrifice after the cure of a patient which are to be found on Epidaurian stelae and which show a particular psychological subtlety: (1) A slave breaks his master's favorite drinking cup. Asclepius "heals" the broken cup, and the master dedicates it to the temple. (2) A poor boy suffering from the stone promises the god his only possession, his much-loved ten knuckle-stones.[48] In this connection I refer again to the sacrifice of Alexander the Great at Gortys. It is noteworthy that the Emperor Claudius decreed that Roman slaves who had been healed by Asclepius at his temple on Tiber Island must be given their freedom.[49]

The principal source for the details which I have given about the ritual of incubation is the *Periēgētēs* of Pausanias, his de-

45 The Zeeman effect consists of the magnetic splitting of a spectral line into a triplet – with the undisturbed original line in the middle – or multiplets, and eating has the connotation of assimilating, that is, making conscious.

46 Aristides *Oratio* 38, ΑΣΚΛΗΠΙΑΔΑΙ 24.

47 Preller-Robert, *Griechische Mythologie,* I, 524.

48 Cf. Chr. Blinkenberg, *Miraklerne i Epidauros* (Copenhagen, 1917), p. 22, No. 3.

49 Suetonius v. 25^2.

scription of Greece. Pausanias made several journeys through every part of Greece about A.D. 165. All his statements are based on personal observation. They are among the most reliable sources of information we have about ancient Hellas. How accurate they are can be seen from the following small detail: in describing the quite insignificant city of Halice,[50] Pausanias says that citizens of this city are named as patients on stelae at Epidaurus. The excavations carried out at Epidaurus in 1833 revealed fragments of these stelae, and in 1928 Kavvadias[51] found among these inscriptions the names of three patients whose place of origin was given as Halice. We now possess three entire stelae and fragments of a fourth out of the six which were still to be seen in the time of Pausanias.[52] They originally stood in the neighborhood of the abaton, and they form the second main source of information for the present essay; for they give no less than seventy case histories. Unfortunately these are rather disappointing owing to the fact that they are nearly all rigidly drawn up in accordance with the following pattern: so-and-so came with such and such an illness, slept in the abaton, had the following dream, and, after making a thank offering, went away cured. The inscriptions belong to the second half of the fourth century B.C., but some go back to the fifth century.[53] They are now available in a critical edition by Herzog.[54] In other sanctuaries of Asclepius there are no *Iamata tou Apollōnos kai tou Asklēpiou,* as these inscriptions concerning miraculous cures by Apollo and Asclepius are called. According to Strabo[55] there were such inscriptions at Cos and Tricca, and, according to legend, Hippocrates copied them down and learned his art from

50 Pausanias ii. 36. 1.

51 First publication of the inscriptions on the stelae by P. Kavvadias, *Ephem. archaiol.* (1883).

52 Pausanias ii. 27. 3.

53 Criticism and literature in Hiller von Gärtringen, *IG,* IV^2, 1 (1929), Prolegomena.

54 Rudolf Herzog, "Die Wunderheilungen von Epidauros," *Philologus,* Supplementband XXII (Leipzig, 1931), 3.

55 Strabo viii. 374.

them.[56] I think it is important to note that the men who drew up the inscriptions on the stelae took great care that the reader should not mistake the records of dreams for real events, for they invariably began them with the phrase *edokei* – "it seemed," or "it appeared."

56 *Ibid.* xiv. 357; Pliny *Hist. nat.* xxix. 4.

CHAPTER VI

THE THOLOS

IT IS NOT POSSIBLE to give archaeological details about the structure of the Asclepieia. Although a great many buildings have been excavated, we do not yet know for certain what their functional significance was. Thus, for example, in Epidaurus itself, it is not yet definitely known which of the many buildings was the abaton. One of the most remarkable of these buildings is a circular one with a labyrinthine basement, called the *tholos,*[1] or *thymelē,* "place of the altar or of sacrifice."[2] Similar buildings are to be found in the Asclepieia at Athens and Pergamum. They are still entirely unexplained. Nevertheless, it seems clear today – although some authorities dispute this – that in the tholos at Pergamum, at any rate, the labyrinthine lower story had an artificial stream of water flowing through it.[3] The juxtaposition of the symbols of a labyrinthine building and of running water came up in a dream of the woman patient who had Dream I (with the key word "Epidaurus") and followed immediately after it. It is:

VII. I am in a subterranean building of confusingly complicated design, through which a stream of water flows....

A labyrinth with water flowing through it, exactly resembling in structure the ground plan of the Epidaurian tholos (Plate 10) is described in the first book of Francesco Colonna's *Hypnerotomachia Poliphili,* and there is an illustration of it in the French edition of Beroalde de Verville (Paris, 1600). It leads to a center

1 Pausanias ii. 27. 3. Fiechter, in P.-W., *s.v.* θόλος, thinks that "tholos" is related to Church Slavonic *dolu* = "hole, grave," and Gothic *dal* = "valley."
2 Fensterbusch, P.-W., *s.v.* φυμέλη.
3 Cf. O. Deubner, *Das Asklepieion von Pergamon* (Berlin, 1938), Plan II.

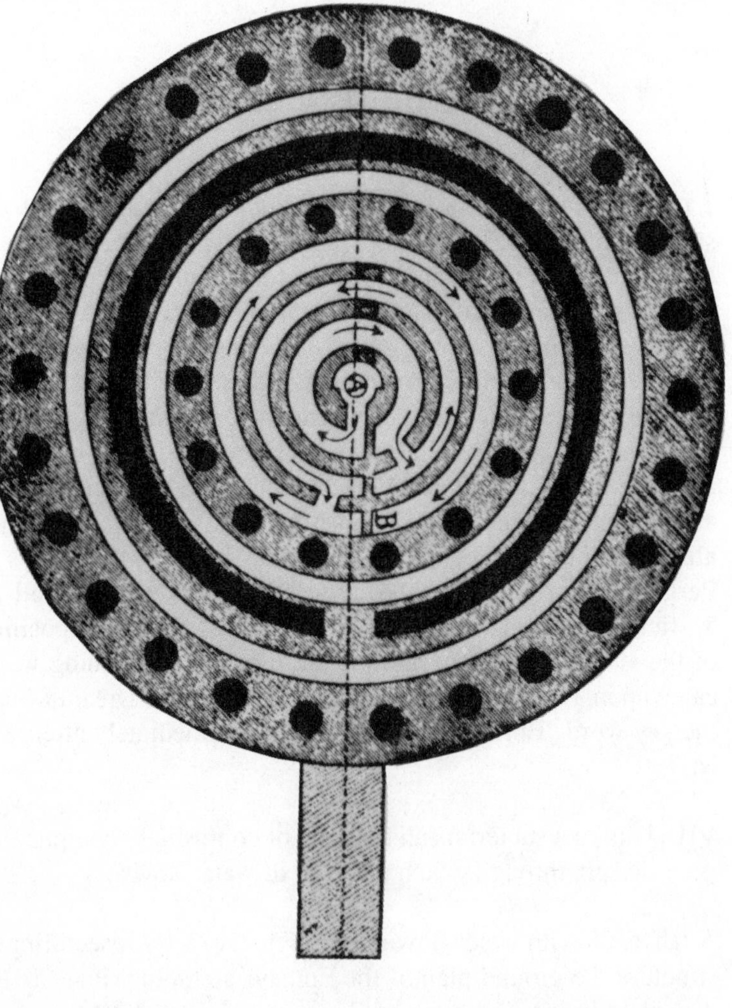

Plate 10
Ground plan of the tholos at Epidaurus. From Plate 2 in Ferdinand Noack, "Der Kernbau der Tholos von Epidauros," *Jahrbuch des deutschen archäologischen Instituts,* XLII (1927), 76 (Berlin, 1928). This plan shows the *classical* labyrinth structure, for which see W.H. Matthews, *Mazes and Labyrinths* (London, 1922).

where there is the inscription *THEŌN LYKOS DYSALGĒTOS*, which is there translated as *Le Loup des Dieux qui est sans pitié*. These examples seem to indicate that the symbol of a labyrinth through which water flows is an autochthonous element in the group of problems which center around incubation.

Water played an important part throughout the cult of Asclepius. It was almost as outstanding a feature as the sacred serpents and dogs. The fountains[4] and bathing pools were never mineral or hot springs, despite a widespread belief to that effect. They simply belonged to Asclepius as a chthonic god, just as his serpent did. It is only through the connection with the god that the spring became a *hagiasma* ("healing spring"). All the *dii chthonii* had a *pēgē* ("spring") in or near their sanctuaries.

In the Asclepieium at Athens, which lies on the southern side of the Acropolis, there is, behind the portico, a grotto hewn out of the rock with a well in it. The Panagia is worshiped there even today. The Christian successors of the ancient gods of healing, the miracle-working saints, nearly always had a spring in their churches. Here I draw the reader's attention to Dream II, in which the spring motif plays a central part. The *numen fontis* is always connected with fertility. Children are born from springs, and the relationship between fertility and healing is evident.[5] I do not know to what extent the nymphaea, so popular in ancient Rome, are connected with these ideas. That the modern Greek feels it is dangerous to sleep beside a spring because the "Nereids" might "seize you or strike you" and make you ill[6] is probably not to be explained, as is commonly assumed, simply by the idea that the nymphs of the ancient world have, owing to Christianization, degenerated into evil water sprites. The archetypal motif of *ho trōsas iasetai* ("whatever wounds heals") is much more likely to be the underlying fundamental reason. This

4 See Pausanias x. 38. 13 and Frazer, *Pausanias*, V, 471, regarding springs.
5 Cf. above, pp. 37-41.
6 B. Schmidt, *Das Volksleben der Neugriechen und das hellenische Altertum* (Leipzig, 1871), p. 119.

view is confirmed by a statement of Juynboll,[7] according to which illness, in the country of Gayos, is thought to be due to the sick person's having unwittingly offended a djinn near a spring.

Owing to the fact that serpents were regarded by the ancients as a symbol of the renewal of life,[8] they are closely connected with the water of life. This is expressed in numerous folk legends.[9] Perhaps the most ancient example of this is to be found in the *Gilgamesh Epic,* Tablet XI. In this passage the snake dwells in the water and eats the herb of life. The herb of life corresponds to the Tree of Life, which in Revelation[10] grows beside the water of life and the leaves of which are for the healing of the nations.[11] An interesting legend is to be found in the Apocalypse of Moses[12] and in the *Vita Adae et Evae.*[13] A remarkable medieval elaboration of this legend is quoted by Wünsche:[14]

> Seth sees in Paradise trees with the most beautiful fruits, and a spring from which the four rivers of Paradise flow. Above the spring there stands a *tree* with branches, but without leaves or bark. It is the Tree of Knowledge, which as a result of the sin of Adam and Eve still bears the marks of God's curse. When Seth looks into Paradise for the second time, he sees that the serpent is wreathed round the bare tree. The third time that he looks into Paradise he sees that the top of the tree reaches up into the sky, and on the top of it there lies a newborn *child* wrapped in swaddling clothes.

7 H.H. Juynboll, *Arch. f. Rel. Wiss.,* VII (1904), 508.
8 Cf. above, p. 20.
9 Cf. Frazer, *Pausanias,* III, 65 ff.
10 Revelation 22:2.
11 Ezekiel 47:1-2.
12 P. Riessler, *Altjüdisches Schrifttum ausserhalb der Bibel* (Augsburg, 1928), p. 138.
13 E. Kautzsch, *Apokryphen und Pseudepigraphen des Alten Testaments,* pp. 516 ff.
14 A. Wünsche, *Die Sagen vom Lebensbaum und Lebenswasser* (Leipzig, 1905).

The theme of healing, which properly belongs to this legend, is present, since the twigs which grew from the seeds of the apples of the Tree of Life were used by Moses for healing. Also these shoots propagated the wood of the Cross, which Solomon had buried deep in the earth after it had refused to fit into the temple as a door beam. Sometime later a pool appeared on this spot, with miraculous healing properties. All the sick who bathed in it were cured.[15]

In Old Persian mythology the spring of life is to be found in an unknown, dark country. Beside it grows the sacred Hom, the tree of immortality.[16] In *Sururi,* in the commentary on Sadi's *Gulistan,* Alexander the Great says:[17] "There is no country left into which I have not been except the *country of darkness,* where, I have been told, is the spring of the water of life."

The legend of the Hesperides is a beautiful example from the ancient world of the relation between tree and serpent. In this legend the serpent Ladon winds itself round the tree which bears the golden apples of the Hesperides.[18]

An etiological connection between the serpent and the healing spring is quite clearly shown by the Soarchus inscription[19] from the Asclepieium at Lebena. It appears from this that Asclepius, in the form of a serpent, showed Soarchus the way to new springs for sanctuaries.[20] The establishment of Asclepieia at Epidaurus Limera[21] and Mantinea[22] was also indicated by serpents. The snake acts also as a guide for Ajax in Philostratus.[23]

15 Cf. Richard Morris, *Legend of the Holy Rood* (London, 1871), and J.H. Philpot, *The Sacred Tree* (London, 1897).
16 F. Windischmann, *Zoroastrische Studien* (Berlin, 1863), pp. 171 ff.
17 A. Wünsche, *op. cit.*, p. 79.
18 See the two illustrations in Roscher, *Lexikon,* I, 2599-2602. Cf. also J. Fergusson, *Tree and Serpent Worship* (London, 1872).
19 Herzog, *WHE,* pp. 53 f.
20 Cf. J.G. Frazer, *Pausanias,* III, 66; W.W. Baudissin, *Studien zur semitischen Religionsgeschichte* (Leipzig, 1876), I, 212 and 239 f., II, 163, No. 8; Gruppe, *Handbuch,* pp. 807 f.; and J.J. Bachofen, *Gräbersymbolik* (Basel, 1954), p. 152.
21 Pausanias iii. 23. 6.
22 *Ibid.* viii. 8. 4.
23 Philostratus *Her.* 706.

In prophecy and the healing art the serpent theme is of course very ancient. Moses' brazen serpents[24] are an example: "Make thee a fiery serpent, and set it upon a pole: and it shall come to pass that everyone ... when he looketh upon it, shall live."

The possession of special medicinal powers by the Naga tribes in Kashmir reminds us of the significance of the Shakti-Kundalini in Tantric Yoga.[25]

In antiquity the serpent generally represents the hero. Cecrops and Erichthonius are examples.[26] Thus Aeneas called the serpent which emerged from the grave of Anchises *geniumve loci famulumve parentis* ("either the tutelary deity of the place or the Familiar Spirit of his father"), which shows that he regarded it as representing the lares of the dead Anchises and thus a salutary phenomenon. The snake here represents the *archēgetai,* "the ancestors of the family." It is well known that reunion with the ancestors means healing.

Melampus, the ancestor of Amphiaraus, learned the art of prophecy from the serpents which he brought up as an expiation for having thoughtlessly killed their parents.[27] According to Plutarch,[28] serpents originate from human corpses; and Pliny[29] explains this idea in more detail by his statement: "Anguem ex medulla hominis spinae gigni accipimus" ("we are told that the serpent sprang from the marrow of a man's backbone"). The snake is thus a metastasis of the human soul. Küster[30] points out that in the ancient world the serpent, as the guardian of graves, watched over the sleep of the dead, and the serpent guarded also the sleep of the living. In view of all this, it is not surprising that Philo Byblos[31] calls the serpent the most spiritual of all animals.

24 Numbers 21:8.
25 Cf. Arthur Avalon, *The Serpent Power* (Madras, 1931).
26 Herodotus viii. 41.
27 Apollodorus i. 9. 11; Aelian *Hist. anim.* xvi. 39 and viii. 12; Aristophanes *Clouds* 507. Cf. also above, p. 41, and the Melampus legend.
28 Plutarch *Cleomenes* 39.
29 Pliny *Hist. nat.* x. 188.
30 Erich Küster, *RGVV*, XIII, 2.
31 Philo Byblos, Frag. 9: πνευματικώτατον γὰρ τὸ ζῷον.

The close connection between snakes and springs is also shown by the fact that the so-called adder of Asclepius is still found today in the *Schlangenbad* (Taunus) where it was introduced by the Romans. The quality of springs as sources of soothsaying and healing is described by Plutarch[32] and Pausanias.[33] We know that tame snakes[34] were kept in Asclepieia, and there seems no doubt that these were tree snakes. This does not conflict with the chthonic significance of the serpents of Asclepius; most of the trees in the hieron were Oriental planes, and it is said of these in ancient texts that the sacred springs flowed out from among their roots; thus here, too, the close connection between trees, snakes and water is preserved. The following example will serve as an analogy:

VIII. I seem to be in Sicily and am walking along a forest path towards a pond surrounded by tall trees so that I can bathe. The occasional tree trunk can be seen in the water. Just as I am getting ready to go swimming I suddenly catch sight of a powerful brown serpent right next to me in the fork of a branch; it is rearing its head. I instinctively recoil and turn away but can see another one on the other side of me and more and more all around until I am surrounded by them; they all seem to have become aware of me. They don't actually threaten me but seem to be looking at me with curiosity. Someone says: yes, well, when you begin analysis, it's a fact that the serpents start to take an interest in you. Scared out of my wits, I wake up.

As far as I am aware, no one has ever considered that the staff of Asclepius might be connected with the tree, although the motif

32 Plutarch *Arist.* xi.

33 Pausanias v. 5. 11; vi. 22. 7; vii. 21. 12. Cf. W.R. Halliday, *Greek Divination* (London, 1913), Chap. VII.

34 Pausanias ii. 28. 1. In any case they were nonpoisonous, as may be seen from Scholiast on Nicander *Theriaca* 438. *Coluber Aesculapii* or *C. longissima,* the "adder of Aesculapius," now *Elaphe longissima,* is probably a different species.

of the tree with a serpent coiled about it is, as we have seen, a very widespread one. Moreover, the statues of Asclepius which have been preserved show the staff resembling a tree trunk more than a walking staff – as many authors would have it. It would be a highly inconvenient staff.[35]

The serpent climbing up the tree symbolizes the process of becoming conscious, as will readily be seen from the legend of Seth's Vision in Paradise.[36] The same meaning attaches to the ascent of the Yoga tree by the Kundalini serpent, which is brought about by the Yoga process.[37]

At this point I hazard a guess which may throw light on a hitherto unexplained passage in Letter 13 of Hippocrates.[38] We read of a festival of the Asclepiads which is called *tēs rhabdou hē analēpsis,* "the lifting up of the staff." Could not the reference perhaps be to the consecration of a medicine man or the granting of a diploma to the doctor by the handing over of the serpent staff?

The fact that the trees in the sanctuaries of Asclepius were particularly sacred can be deduced from the rules for the protection of the sacred grove, which, as was pointed out above, gave its name to the entire sacred precinct. These rules are to be found on Stelae 11 and 12 at Cos.[39] Arguing from analogy, it seems probable that the trees served as *Lappenbäume* (trees or shrubs in Yugoslavia on which wound dressings are hung in order that the disease may be transferred to the tree[40]). An Epidaurian example of transference to the bandages may be found in Miracle VI:[41]

Pandarus, a Thessalian who had marks on his forehead. In

35 Cf. Plate 3 and especially Plate 5.
36 Cf. p. 64.
37 Cf. p. 65.
38 Hippocrates *Epid.* xiii (ed. Kühn, 778).
39 Herzog, "Heilige Gesetze von Kos."
40 P. Kemp, *Healing Ritual* (London, 1935). Kemp gives an abundance of interesting material from the Balkans in modern times which bears comparison with the ancient rite of incubation. For older sources see p. 75, n. 3, in Weinreich, *AHW*.
41 Herzog, *WHE*.

> his healing sleep he saw a vision. He dreamed that the god bound up the marks with a bandage and commanded him, when he left the sacred hall, to take off the bandage and to dedicate it to the temple. When day came, he rose and took off the bandage, and found his face free from the marks; but the bandage he dedicated in the temple, it bore the marks of the forehead.

I believe the original meaning of the term "transference" lies in this idea.

The important part played by water in the Asclepieia has yet another aspect. Large quantities of water were needed to keep the pools filled. The baths which were prescribed for incubants had, as previously said, the significance of lustrations, through which the soul was freed from contamination by the body. This enabled the incubant to have dream experiences without restriction. In this sense the bath is *oneiraiteton* ("dream-producing"), an expression frequently used in the magical papyri. It is clear that in this way a healing dream can occur.

In addition the bath has the meaning of a *voluntaria mors,* a voluntary death, and of a rebirth.[42] In other words, it has a baptismal aspect. As we know from Pollux,[43] the bath, in the form of the bridal bath, has the meaning of a preliminary condition for marriage as initiation or mystery. Marriage was regarded in the ancient world as an initiation into the mysteries, for which reason unmarried persons had a jug (*loutrophoros*) placed on their graves. The idea was that in the next world they would use it to carry water for their bridal bath.[44] It will be seen that the bath is here brought into close connection with the idea of the *hieros gamos* ("sacred nuptials") as the *mysterium coniunctionis*.[45] We will consider below the extent to which the healing process in the

42 Cf. pp. 64-66.
43 Pollux *Onom.* iii. 43.
44 Demosthenes xxxxiv. 18 and 30; Eustathius on *Iliad* xxiii. 141. Cf. also J.G. Frazer, *Pausanias,* V, 388-391.
45 Cf. pp. 97-98.

Asclepian sanctuaries was regarded as *synousia* ("coitus") with the god.

In this context an archaeological detail about the Asclepian sanctuary at Epidaurus is of particular interest from the psychological point of view. It has come down to us from a literary source only, but that source is Pausanias and is therefore especially reliable. He tells us[46] of paintings in the cupola of the tholos at Epidaurus. These paintings represented two figures: the first was a personification of Intoxication, drinking from a crystal goblet through which her face could be seen; the second was Eros, who had thrown away his bows and arrows and in place of them held a lyre.

In the temple of Asclepius at Cos there was, according to Cicero,[47] a statue of Venus Anadyomene by Apelles; this was later brought to Rome by Augustus. Although we know nothing about the function of the tholos, its situation alone shows that it must have played an important part in the ritual of the Asclepieium. The Epidaurian tholos was moreover the most beautiful round building in the whole of Greece and was built by Polyclitus,[48] the most famous architect of the day. The pictures were painted by Pausias the Younger and thus date from the middle of the fourth century B.C. The tholos took twenty-one years to build, and enormous sums were paid to the builders and artists; an exact account is extant. For the purpose of the present study, however, it is the paintings which are of special interest: the intoxication of the soul, and Eros, who has renounced his dangerous weapons and is making music instead. These are very obscure symbols, but I nevertheless venture upon an interpretation, asking the reader to regard it simply as a suggestion or a stimulus to speculation, for it is a daring conjecture.

The pair of opposites, woman-man, here contains a further typological opposition: the Dionysian, represented by intoxication, and the Apollonian, represented by music. To my mind, the

46 Pausanias ii. 27. 3.
47 Cicero *De divin.* i. 13. 23.
48 Pausanias ii. 27. 1.

figure of Methe (Intoxication) represented orgiastic corybantism, and the lyre-playing Eros its cure. Corybantism was a state of religious possession which appeared in the Dionysian thiasos. To the Greeks, however, music had the power of counteracting sickness. Orpheus, the great singer, claimed, according to Pausanias,[49] to have been the first to discover purification from impious actions and in consequence the healing of disease (*nosōn te iamata*). Orpheus was, according to most accounts, torn to pieces by the Bacchantes in a Dionysian frenzy. In the *Bassarai* of Aeschylus this is said to have been brought about by Dionysus because Orpheus sacrificed to his enemy Apollo. Orpheus thus perished as a result of the Apollonian-Dionysian opposition.

The mythical musician Thaletas, according to Pratinas,[50] rid Sparta of a terrible epidemic by his irresistible playing on the *aulos* (flute). We should not forget either that Chiron, the medical instructor of Asclepius, also taught music: *kai iatrous apephaine kai mousikous hērmotte kai dikaious epoiei*[51] ("he educated them to be physicians and turned their minds to music and made them into just men"). It is a well-known fact that physicians today are frequently fond of music. It was Chiron who taught Achilles to play the lyre.[52]

We know from Plato[53] and Aristotle that the Greeks made therapeutic use of music in order to cure[54] the so-to-speak drunken *korybantiōntes* of their Dionysian frenzy by means of catharsis. But the Dionysian is the dark side of the Apollonian and is very closely bound up with prophecy. When Apollo took possession of the oracle of Delphi, he first had to drive out the previous occupant, Dionysus. Later, however, he made peace with him. The tomb of Dionysus was shown in the temple of Apollo at Delphi, and the front pediment of Apollo's own temple

49 *Ibid.* ix. 30. 3.
50 In Plutarch *De musica* 42.
51 Philostratus *Heroicus* 9.
52 Scholiast on Caes. German. Aratea 291, and Lucius Ampelius *Liber memorialis* 2. 9.
53 Plato *Ion* 533 E-534 A; *Laws* vii. 790 D-E.
54 Cf. E. Rohde, *Psyche*², II, 47-49.

bore the image of Apollo, while the back one showed the ecstatic, nocturnal Dionysus. The close relation which came to exist between Dionysus and Apollo is also clearly shown in the interchangeability of their attributes.[55] Even the cult name Paean is transferred to Dionysus, although not the Apollonian paean but rather the dithyramb belongs to him.[56] The Dionysian and the Apollonian cry are actually amalgamated in the Delphic paean of Philodamus of Scarphea:[57] *euoi ō io Bakch' ō ie Paian.*

According to Arnobius,[58] the *vindemia,* the vintage, is sacred to Asclepius, and prayers for the good health of the people are said at that time. The vintage closed with the festival of the Meditrinalia (October 11),[59] from which the existence of a goddess Meditrina has been deduced, who would certainly have to do with health.[60] Varro[61] records the following toast used at this festival: *Novum vetus vinum bibo, novo veteri morbo medeor* ("I, an old man, drink new wine; I heal an old sickness with a new one").

It appears from Plutarch[62] that similar prayers for good health were said at the Athenian *Pithoigia* (festival of the tapping of the wine casks, *pithoi*) at the time of the Dionysian Anthesteria. Gruppe[63] emphasizes the relationship between Dionysus and Asclepius, taking as an example the statue of Calamis. It can be proved that Dionysus was a very ancient god of healing at Delphi, where his oracle was supplanted by Apollo's.[64] The chief festival of Asclepius at Athens took place on the day after the Lenaea and before the Great Dionysia,[65] and his sanctuary

55 Cf. F.A. Voigt in Roscher, *Lexikon,* I, 1033.
56 Euripides, Frag. 480 (ed. Nauck); *Orphic Hymns* 52. 11.
57 Cf. *Bull. hell.,* XIX (1895), 391.
58 Arnobius vii. 32.
59 Cf. Georg Wissowa, *Kult,* p. 115.
60 Cf. Paulus, *ex Festo,* p. 123, 16.
61 Varro *Lingua Latina* vi. 21.
62 Plutarch *Quaest. conviv.* iii. 7. 1.
63 Gruppe, *Handbuch,* p. 1449.
64 F.A. Voigt in Roscher, *Lexikon, s.v.* "Dionysos," 1033.
65 Aristotle *Res publ. Athen.* 56. 4.

was next to the great Theater of Dionysus.[66] On the island of Cos, too, the pentaeteric *megala Asklēpieia* (the great festivals of Asclepius) with musical competitions took place at the same time as the Dionysia.[67] It is quite clear from Plato[68] that musical and poetic competitions on a large scale took place at the Asclepieia. The practice was probably taken over from the worship of Apollo. The particularly magnificent theaters in the sanctuaries are further evidence of the importance attached to the influence of music in ancient ritual healing.

It can therefore be concluded without straining the evidence that the mitigated Dionysian orgy, the "sober drunkenness" (*methē nēphalios*), or intoxication of the soul, on the one hand, and music, representing the Apollonian transformation of Eros, on the other, belonged to the mantic nature of incubation. The erotic function here had an exclusively lytic significance and thus brought healing. The throwing away of bow and arrows indicates that Eros renounced the dangerous projection of the emotions in favor of music in the Asclepieium, which, according to the characteristic Greek view of the matter, purifies men from the passions. The reader may be reminded of a passage in Plato's *Republic*:[69]

> Then, Glaucon, I said, is not musical education of paramount importance for those reasons, because rhythm and harmony enter most powerfully into the innermost part of the soul and lay forcible hands upon it, bearing grace with them, so making graceful him who is rightly trained?

Plutarch[70] also alludes to the lytic effect of music:

> We need only remember Terpander, who once quelled a

66 Marinus *Vita Procli* c. 29.
67 W. Dittenberger, *Sylloge*, 398, 13, and *Bull. de corresp. hellén.*, CCXI, 16.
68 Plato *Ion* 530 A.
69 Plato *Rep.* iii. 401 D.
70 Plutarch *De musica* 42.

riot amongst the Lacedaemonians, and Thaletas of Crete, who, as Pratinas writes, was once called in by the Lacedaemonians on the advice of the Pythian oracle, and healed them and rid Sparta of the plague which raged there.

Cicero,[71] Seneca[72] and Catullus[73] prove, moreover, that Phrygian music in particular had a rousing effect and thus produced that enthusiasm in which the soul becomes capable of soothsaying. Galen[74] confirms the notion of the Aristotelian catharsis when he says that Asclepius commanded many persons to write odes or mimes and to compose certain songs, because the movement of their emotions had become too violent and raised the temperature of their bodies in an unwholesome way.[75] The Stoic Cleanthes, according to Philodemus of Gadara,[76] said that "examples in poetry and music are even better than the logos of philosophy, which indeed can make things human and divine sufficiently known, but is prosaic and therefore is really an unsuitable means for expression of divine things; so that measures (of verse), songs (melodies) and rhythms come as near as is possible to the truth of the contemplation of the divine."

One of the few pieces of information that have come down to us about the rites practiced in the Asclepieia is that music was played in them.[77] Choruses in particular are mentioned.[78] The paean is a song accompanied by the cithara; later the flute was added.[79] Paean was, however, also an epithet of Apollo and his son Asclepius as well as of other gods. In Homer, Apollo is the god of health and sickness, while the divine physician in the *Iliad* is called Paean (*Paian* or *Poiēōn*). In this capacity he heals

71 Cicero *De divin.* i. 114.
72 Seneca *Ep.* 108.
73 Catullus 63. 20-29.
74 Galen *De sanit. tuenda* i. 8. 19-20.
75 Cf. E. Frank, *Plato und die sogenannten Pythagoraeer* (Halle, 1923), pp. 1 ff.
76 Philodemus *De musica* IV. XXVIII, 1 (ed. Joh. Kemke [Leipzig, 1884], pp. 97 f.).
77 Athenaeus *Deipnosophistae* xiv. 7. 617 b.
78 *IG*, IV^2, Nos. 40 and 41.
79 Cf. below, p. 87.

Hades[80] and Ares.[81]

A modern parallel to the importance of song is found in the following dream of an analysand:

IX. I am in a room where an operation is to be performed, I think by Professor Jung. It turns out that a group of medical students are to hear a lecture about a particular operation which is described as "biological." Before it begins, everyone stands up and sings a hymn. When this is finished, I am apparently not quite familiar with the customary practice, and continue with *Gloria Patri et Filio et Spiritu Sancto*. I notice at once, however, that this ought not to come at the end of the hymn and am rather embarrassed until a surgeon who is standing near me smiles and tells me that I need not worry about it, because many people have made the same mistake. The song appears to be the school hymn.

In connection with the use of song in the sanctuaries we should also remember the equation *logos* = *pharmakon* = *iatros* (word = medicine = physician).[82] The texts of the Epidaurian school hymns have been edited by Maas.[83]

To return, after this digression, to the ritual of incubation in the stricter sense, it is important, from the point of view with which we are concerned, to make it clear that the decisive event took place at night. The cure occurred in the abaton during the night, whether the patient actually slept or stayed awake from excitement. In the latter case it was effected not by the dream but by a vision. This is further proof that the Asclepian miraculous healing was regarded as a mystery; for all the mysteries were celebrated at night.

80 *Iliad* v. 401.
81 *Ibid.* v. 900.
82 Cf. E. Howald, *Hermes,* LIV (1919), 187 ff.
83 P. Maas, "Epidaurische Hymnen," *Schriften der Königsberger Gelehrten Gesellschaft, Geisteswissenschaftliche Klasse,* IX, V (1932).

Incubation was by no means peculiar to the cult of Asclepius. Indeed it was far older than his cult, and by comparing it with its more primitive predecessors we can learn much that is unknown to us in connection with Asclepius himself.

CHAPTER VII

INCUBATION AT THE ORACLE OF TROPHONIUS

THE RITUAL OF INCUBATION was widespread. In Homer[1] the Selloi or Helloi lay on the ground on earthen beds and had dreams which they interpreted prophetically. Herodotus[2] says that the Nasamoni, a Libyan race which dwelt in the neighborhood of Mount Atlas, slept on the graves of their ancestors in order to have dreams. Tertullian[3] states that the same was true of the Celts. It will be remembered that Isaiah[4] describes a similar proceeding: the Septuagint uses the expression *koimōntai dia enypnia* ("they spend the nights for the sake of dreams"). According to Strabo[5] people slept on the skins of the sacrificed animals – black rams – at the oracle of Calchas on Mount Drion in Daunium in order to have healing dreams. At the foot of the mountain there was a temple of Podalirius, the son of Asclepius. This was also done at the oracle of Faunus, according to Vergil.[6] The underlying idea seems to be that of contact with *potnia Cthōn,* Sacred Mother Earth, who sends the dreams.[7]

If the interpretation of M. Komosko[8] is correct, incubation can be traced back to the third millennium B.C. Komosko believes, however, that a basic difference exists between incubation practiced with the exclusive aim of experiencing a theophany, as is the case in the Gudea cylinder, and incubation practiced in

1 *Iliad* xvi. 233.
2 Herodotus iv. 172.
3 Tertullian *De anima* 57 (Tresp. 142).
4 Isaiah 65:4.
5 Strabo vi. 3. 9.
6 Vergil *Aeneid* vii. 86 ff.
7 Euripides *Hec.* 70, *Iph. in T.* 1231.
8 M. Komosko, "Eine uralte Beschreibung der 'Inkubation' (Gudea-Cylinder A VIII, 1-14)," *Zeitschr. f. Assyriologie,* XXIX (1914), 158-71.

order to heal sickness. I think in view of what has been said above that this distinction cannot be maintained. Witzel,[9] a critic of Komosko's, at least agrees with him that this is a case of an incubation ritual.

Strabo[10] speaks of a temple of Pluto between Tralles and Nyssa where the sick stayed in a village not far from Charon's cave. The priests incubated for them (*enkoimōntes hyper autōn*), invoked Hera Catachthonia and Pluto, and had dreams indicating the cause and cure of the sickness (*tas therapeias*). Sometimes the priests brought the sick into the cave. Others were not allowed access. The afflicted remained there quietly for several days without eating. They then had dreams themselves, but made use of the priests as mystagogues – here simply dream interpreters. We have, however, fuller details about the ritual in the equally ancient and primitive rites of the chthonic heroes Amphiaraus and Trophonius, who were also worshiped in the temples of Asclepius.

As regards Amphiaraus,[11] a ram was first sacrificed at Oropus for the purpose of purification; the sick person then lay down on its skin and awaited the healing dream. Amphiaraus dwelt also in his fountain,[12] into which silver and gold coins were thrown as offerings. (We are reminded here of the Trevi Fountain in Rome.) I myself found coins in the fountain of Trophonius (see later) at Livadia (ancient Lebadea) some years ago.

It is Trophonius, however, with whom we are chiefly concerned. In Frazer[13] we possess a great deal of literary evidence from the ancient world about the incubatorium of Trophonius at Lebadea. A detailed description is given by Samter,[14] and the

9 M. Witzel, "Zur Inkubation bei Gudea," *Zeitschr. f. Assyriologie,* XXX (1915), 101.
10 Strabo xiv. 1. 44.
11 *Ibid.* ix. 399; Pausanias i. 34. 2-5; also Frazer, *Pausanias,* II, 466 ff.
12 Pausanias i. 34 ff.
13 Frazer, *Pausanias,* V, 199 ff. (archaeology).
14 E. Samter, *Die Religion der Griechen,* pp. 40 ff.

subject is treated in very great detail by van Dale.[15] I shall confine myself mainly to Pausanias,[16] since his information is based on personal observation: he himself was initiated. Trophonius, like Asclepius, had the serpent as one of his attributes. The cock was also sacred to both. Trophonius' statue by Praxiteles at Lebadea was similar to that of Asclepius. According to Cicero[17] they have a common ancestry: Trophonius is a half-brother of Asclepius, being the son of Ischys (Valens) and Persephone (Coronis). In one account he is also the son of Apollo, or an illegitimate child of Epicaste. Asclepius, too, was illegitimate. One of the names given to Zeus is "Trophonius,"[18] and a group of sculptures in the cave of Hercyna at Lebadea, which was believed to represent Asclepius and Hygieia because the figures had serpent staffs, is explained by Pausanias as representing Trophonius and Hercyna. His cave was the one in which he was born and where, like Zeus, he was fed on honey. Here his serpents dwelled. The sanctuary was thus in essence a cave (*katabasion*). It seems clear from a passage in Isyllus of Epidaurus[19] that a catabasis into the abaton was originally required in the cult of Asclepius, too. In any case Asclepius had a cave sanctuary with a cold spring at Zarax near Epidaurus.[20]

Anyone who wished to consult Trophonius in his cave had first to spend several days in a house consecrated to the Agathos Daimon and Agathe Tyche (Good Demon and Good Luck) and during this time had to observe rules for purification and abstain from warm baths. On the other hand, he had to bathe in the cold river Hercyna (Hercyna here is the *numen fontis;* Demeter is also called Hercyna). Many animals were sacrificed to Trophonius and his children as well as to Zeus, Apollo and Demeter, and their flesh was eaten. Demeter was also a goddess of healing at

15 Antonius van Dale, *De oraculis veterum ethnicorum dissertationes duae* (Amsterdam, 1700).
16 Pausanias ix. 39. 2 ff.
17 Cicero *De nat. deorum* iii. 22. 56.
18 Strabo ix. 2. 38.
19 *IG,* IV^2, I, No. 1288; III, 27-31.
20 Pausanias ii. 24. 2.

Eleusis,[21] as is shown by a votive relief of Eucrates dating from the beginning of the fourth century B.C.[22] Apellas was commanded to sacrifice to the Eleusinian goddesses.[23] A particularly beautiful epigram by Antiphilus[24] runs:

> My staff guided me to the temple uninitiated not only in the mysteries, but in the sunlight. The goddesses initiated me into both, and on that night I knew that my eyes as well as my soul had been purged of night. I went back to Athens without a staff, proclaiming the holiness of the mysteries of Demeter more clearly with my eyes than with my tongue.

The frequency with which diseases of the eyes are referred to in ancient reports of miraculous cures is also noticeable in the Epidaurian *iamata*. In reality trachoma was widespread in the Middle East. However, the deities gave "sight" to men in quite another sense by their miraculous help. The above-quoted epigram bears witness to this. Persephone *cheirogonia* ("midwife")[25] was, according to Gruppe[26] and Preller-Robert,[27] also a goddess of birth (cf. the parallel between healing and giving birth, pp. 101-103).

The priest of Trophonius saw from the entrails of the sacrificed animals whether or not the moment for the *katabasis* ("descent") had arrived. The haruspicy of the last sacrifice, a black ram, was decisive. If it turned out favorably, the person who wished to consult the oracle was called during the night by two thirteen-year-old boys, known as Hermae, was led to the river Hercyna, and was there anointed and bathed. The priests

21 Cf. O. Rubensohn, "Demeter als Heilgöttin," *Mitt. d. arch. Inst. in Athen*, XX (1895), 360-67.
22 *Ephem. archaiol.* (1892), pp. 133 ff., Plate V; quoted from Kern, *Religion*, II, 205.
23 Cf. Herzog, *WHE*, pp. 43 f.
24 Antiphilus, *Palatine Anthology* ix. 298.
25 Hesychius, *s.v.* χειρογονία.
26 Gruppe, *Handbuch*, II, 860, n. 2.
27 Preller-Robert, *Griechische Mythologie*, I, 781.

then led him to two springs, Lethe and Mnemosyne, which flowed out quite near each other. After drinking from these, he forgot everything that had been on his mind until then, and he received the power to remember what he was about to see when he made his descent. We are reminded here of St. Paul's Letter to the Philippians (3:13), which reads, with respect to the needed *metanoia* (change of heart): *hen de, ta men opisō epilanthanomenos tois de emprosthen epekteinomenos, kata skopon diōkō* ... (Septuagint); or, in the Vulgate: "unum autem: quae sunt priora, extendens meipsum ad destinatum persequor..." ("but this *one* thing I *do*: forgetting those things which are behind, and reaching forth unto those things which are before...").

At this point I quote a fantasy of a woman patient because of the numerous remarkable parallels which it presents to the symbolism of these ancient incubation rituals:

X. I had lost my way in a wood and was very hungry and thirsty. Suddenly I saw a bright light through the trees, and I could see something golden shining. I went toward it and came to a bright meadow in which there stood a great apple tree with golden fruit. Full of hope, I tried to pluck an apple, but I could not succeed, for whenever I grasped at one, the branch bent away from me. I sat down sadly under the tree and began to weep. Suddenly I heard above my head a bird singing a most beautiful song. There was a rustling above me, and suddenly the bird was before me. It was a very beautiful creature, with feathers of all colors. It asked me why I was weeping, and I told it how hungry and thirsty I was.

"Come with me to my master, and he will give you food and drink," said the bird. I followed the bird as fast as I could, although I did not know where it was leading me. Soon we came to a golden gate. Before we went in, the bird came to me again and gave me one of the golden apples which it had plucked from the tree and brought along, and also a blue feather which it plucked from its own plumage. Then the bird said, "Take these things, perhaps later they will be useful to you; but do not eat the apple now, for now you are going to receive other food."

Then we went through the gate, and I *forgot everything* that had happened before, and all my past life. I followed the bird, which led me through a wonderful garden to a golden castle. On the steps there stood a young man, all shining, in a white garment and wearing a golden crown. He came to meet me.

"That is the King, your bridegroom," said the bird; and to the king he said, "Here is your bride, whom I bring to you."

I took all this for granted, for I no longer remembered that I was already married. The King had sent the bird to find the first woman who stood under the tree with the golden apples that day, for she was to be his bride; and I was that woman. We went into the castle together; everything was splendidly decorated, and the wedding breakfast was already set out; and I ate, and restored the strength of my weary body.

I then lived with the King as his wife for I do not know how long. His love made me happy. I lived free from care in magnificent, enchanted surroundings; I always had everything that I wanted, and it never occurred to me that it could be otherwise. At last I had a child who was as beautiful and resplendent as his father.

Shortly after the child was born, however, I woke up during the night and felt very thirsty. At the same time I heard the many-colored bird, whose voice I recognized, singing a plaintive song in the garden. Then I thought of the golden apple which the bird had given me; perhaps that would quench my thirst. I got up quietly and got it out of the cupboard in which I had put it. As soon as I had taken the first bite, *I suddenly remembered all my past life before the time when I had been led into the enchanted castle,* and I felt a great longing for my husband and child. I fled as fast as I

> could; I felt my way softly out of the room and down the stairs and into the garden. But when I came to the golden gate, it was locked fast. Was I a prisoner? Then from the distance I heard my bird singing his song. This reminded me of his blue feather, which luckily I had with me. I touched the gate with it, and it sprang open. I was now outside; but what direction must I go to reach home? I laid the feather on the ground, and it turned towards the east, so I went in that direction. Every time I was uncertain which way to go I laid it down, and it showed me the way until at last I came home to my husband and child.

Amnesia is an essential condition if the patient is to give himself up completely to the experience of incubation. This is in direct contrast to the high valuation of anamnesis which prevails elsewhere in medicine. Here, anamnesis applies exclusively to the unconscious experiences which are visualized during incubation, and its purpose is to make them accessible to consciousness and reality and also to make it possible to utilize them.

After the incubant consulting Trophonius had drunk from the two springs, he was shown the statue of the god, which was supposed to be by Daedalus and was never shown to anyone but incubants. The incubant was then clothed in white linen and wrapped in bands like a child in swaddling clothes.[28] Next he was given a ladder so that he could climb down into the cave. When he reached the bottom, he had to creep feet foremost into a hole which was only just big enough to allow a human body through. When he was in as far as the knees, he was sucked right in, as if by a mighty whirlpool. In his hands he held honey cakes, which he fed to the serpents living there, to propitiate them.

The *mazas memagmenas meliti*[29] correspond to the *pelanos,* a cake or piece of dough made of fine flour mixed with honey and

28 Cf. below, p. 101.
29 Pausanias ix. 39. 11.

poppy seed,[30] and are a typical offering to serpents. These cakes are also identical with the *offa* which the Sibyl gives to Cerberus in Vergil.[31]

The incubant then heard or saw his oracle. Sometimes he came up again the next day, but sometimes he was *kept* down below for several days. The anabasis, or rather the being-thrust-out-again through the hole, which Pausanias compares to an oven, was again feet foremost. Let us recall at this point that the popular custom still exists of carrying the deceased out of the house feet first, which is probably connected with the identity of death and rebirth. In Jewish necromancy the same motif recurs in that the spirit that is being conjured up rises from the grave feet first.

The curious fact that the incubant in his catabasis was drawn into the cave feet foremost is readily explicable if one remembers that what takes place is a birth in reverse. What is more difficult to understand is that in the anabasis, which certainly represents a birth process in a forward direction, the feet again come first. Perhaps the following information given by Frazer[32] may throw light on this peculiar circumstance: In the Punjab a first child born with the feet forward was considered to have healing powers.[33] Similarly it was believed in the northeast of Scotland that those born with their feet first possessed great power to heal all kinds of sprains, lumbago and rheumatism, either by rubbing the affected part or by trampling on it.[34] The chief virtue lay in the feet.

When the incubant came up, he was placed on the throne of Mnemosyne, where he was able to remember all that he had

30 R. Herzog, "Aus dem Asklepieion von Kos," *Arch. Rel. Wiss.*, X (1907), 201-28 and 400-15.

31 Vergil *Aeneid* vi. 419-21; cf. Frazer, *Pausanias,* II, 183.

32 J.G. Frazer, *The Golden Bough: A Study in Magic and Religion* (12 vols.; 3rd ed.; London, 1917-18), VII/I, 295 f.

33 *Census of India, 1911*, Vol. XIV, *Punjab,* Part I (Report by Pandit Harikishan Kaul) (Lahore, 1912), p. 302.

34 Rev. Walter Gregor, *Notes on the Folk-Lore of the North-East of Scotland* (London, 1881), pp. 45 f.

experienced and relate it to the priests, who made careful records of all that he said. The "case history" was dedicated in the temple. The incubant was then handed over to his friends; he was still quite unconscious and trembling all over. His friends took him to the temple of the Agathos Daimon and Agathe Tyche again. There he gradually recovered, and the power of laughing returned to him. Obviously there was no laughing down below! This reminds us of the Eleusinian *agelastos petra* ("laugh-depriving stone"), which was also an entry into Hades, and the catabasis to Trophonius was understood in this way. It should be noted here that Trophonius was equated with Hermes *katachthonios* ("of the underworld"). In ancient Greece they said of an overserious man:[35] *eis Trophōniou memanteutai,* "He has paid a visit to Trophonius!"

An account given by Hippocrates[36] shows that the apparitions of Asclepius could be terrifying; but the methods used in consulting Trophonius were much more drastic and more primitive. A detailed account may be found in a passage from Plutarch,[37] which is quoted in full:

> Timarchus ... greatly wished to know what was really meant by the Divine Sign [*daimonion* in Greek] of Socrates, and so, like a generous youth fresh to the taste of Philosophy, having taken no one but Cebes and myself [Simmias] into his plan, went down into the cave of Trophonius, after performing the usual rites of the oracle. Two nights and one day he remained below; and when most people had given him up, and his family was mourning for him, at early dawn he came very radiant. He knelt to the God, then made his way at once through the crowd, and related to us many wonderful things which he had seen and heard.
>
> 22. He said that, when he descended into the oracular

35 Suidas, *s.v.* εἰς Τροφωνίου μεμάντευται.
36 Hippocrates *Epid.* xv (IX, p. 340, 1 ff. L).
37 Plutarch *De genio Socrat.* 22 f.

chamber, he first found himself in a great darkness; then, after a prayer, lay a long while not very clearly conscious whether he was awake or dreaming; only he fancied that his head received a blow, while a dull noise fell on his ears, and then the sutures parted and allowed his soul to issue forth. As it passed upwards, rejoicing to mingle with the pure, transparent air, it appeared first to draw a long deep breath, after its narrow compression, and to become larger than before, like a sail as it is filled out. Then he heard dimly a whirring noise overhead, out of which came a sweet voice. He looked up and saw land nowhere, only islands shining with lambent fire, from time to time changing color with one another, as though it were a coat of dye, while the light became spangled in the transition. They appeared to be countless in number and in size enormous, not all equal but all alike circular. He thought that as these moved around there was an answering hum of the air, for the gentleness of that voice which was harmonized out of all corresponded to the smoothness of the motion. Through the midst of the islands a sea or lake was interfused, all shining with the colors as they were commingled over its grey surface. Some few islands floated in a straight course and were conveyed across the current; many others were drawn on by the flood, being almost submerged. The sea was of great depth in some parts towards the south, but there were very shallow reaches, and it often swept over places and then left them dry, having no strong ebb. The color was in places pure as that of the open sea, in others turbid and marshlike. As the islands passed through the surf, they never came round to their starting point again or described a circle, but slightly varied their points of impact, thus describing a continuous spiral as they went round. The sea was inclined to the approximate middle and highest part of the encompassing firmament by a little less than eight-ninths of the whole, as it appeared to him. It had two openings which received rivers of fire pouring in from opposite sides, so that it was lashed into foam, and its grey surface was turned to white. This he saw, delighted at the spectacle; but as he turned his eyes downwards, there appeared a chasm, vast and round as though hewn out of a sphere; it was strangely terrible and full of utter darkness, not in repose but often agitated and surging up; from which were heard roarings innumerable and groanings of beasts, and wailings of innumerable infants, and with these mingled cries of men and women, dim sounds of all sorts, and turmoils sent up indistinctly from the distant depth, to his no small consternation. Time passed, and an unseen person said to him, "Timarchus, what do you wish to learn?" "Everything," he replied, "for all is wonderful." "We," the voice said, "have little to do with the regions above; they belong to other Gods; but the province of Persephone, which we administer, being one of the four which Styx bounds, you may survey if you will." To his question, "What is Styx?" "A way to Hades," was the reply, "and it passes right opposite, parting the light at its very vertex, but reaching up, as you see, from Hades below; where it touches the light in its revolution it marks off the remotest region of all. Now, there are four first principles of all things, the first of life, the second of motion, the third of birth, the fourth of death. The first is linked to the second by Unity, in the Unseen: the second to the third by Mind, in the sun: the third to the fourth by Nature, in the moon. Over each of these combinations a Fate, daughter of Necessity, presides, and holds the keys; of the first Atropos, of the second, Clotho, of the one belonging to the moon, Lachesis, and the turning-point of birth is there. For the other islands contain Gods, but the moon, which belongs to earthly spirits, only avoids Styx by a slight elevation, and is caught once in one hundred and seventy-seven secondary measures. As Styx moves upon her, the souls cry aloud in terror; for many slip from off her and are caught by Hades. Others the moon bears upwards from below, as they turn towards her; and for these death coincides with the moment of birth, those excepted which are guilty and impure, and which are not allowed to approach her while she lightens and bellows fearfully, mourning for their own fate as they slip away and are borne downwards for another birth, as you see." "But I see nothing," said Timarchus, "save many stars quivering around the gulf, others sinking into it, others again darting up from below." "Then you see the spirits themselves," the voice said, "though you do not know it. It is thus: every soul partakes of mind, there is none irrational or mindless; but so much of soul as is mingled with flesh and with affections is altered and turned towards the irrational by its sense of pleasures and pains. But the mode of mingling is not the same for every soul. Some are merged entirely into body, and are disturbed by passions throughout their whole being during life. Others are in part mixed up with it, but leave outside their purest part, which is not drawn in, but is like a life buoy which floats on the surface, and touches the head of one who has sunk into the depth, the soul clinging around it and being kept upright, while so much of it is supported as obeys and is not overmastered by the affections. The part which is borne below the surface within the body is called soul. That which is left free from dissolution most persons call mind, taking it to be something inside themselves, resembling the reflected images in mirrors; but those who are rightly informed know that it is outside themselves and address it as a spirit. The stars, Timarchus," the voice went on, "which you see extinguished, you are to think of as souls entirely merged in bodies; those which give light again and shine from below upwards, shaking off, as though it were mud, a sort of gloom and dimness, are those which sail up again out of their bodies after death; those which are parted upwards are spirits, and belong to men who are said to have understanding. Try to see clearly in each the bond by which it coheres with soul!" Hearing this, he paid closer attention himself, and saw the stars tossing about, some less, some more, as we see the corks which mark out nets in the sea move over its surface; but some, like the shuttles used in weaving, in entangled and irregular figures, not able to settle the motion into a straight line. The voice said that those who kept a straight and orderly movement were men whose souls had been well broken in by fair nurture and training and did not allow their irrational part to be too harsh and rough. Those which often inclined upwards and downwards in an irregular and confused manner, like horses plunging off from a halter, were fighting against the yoke which tempers the disobedient and ill-trained for want of education; sometimes getting the mastery and swerving round to the right; again bent by passions and drawn on to share in sins, then again resisting and putting force upon them. The coupling bond, like a curb set on the irrational part of the soul whenever it resists, brings on repentance, as we call it, for sins, and shame for all lawless and intemperate pleasures, being really a pain and a stroke inflicted by it on the soul when it is bitten by that which masters and rules it, until at length, being thus punished, it becomes obedient to the rein and familiar with it, and then, like a tame creature, without blow or pain, understands the spirit quickly by signs and hints. These then are led, late in the day and by slow degrees, to their duty. Out of those who are docile and obedient to their spirit from their first birth, is formed the prophetic and inspired class, to which belonged the soul of Hermodorus of Clazomenae, of which you have surely heard; how it would leave the body entirely and wander over a wide range by night and by day and then come back again, having been present where many things were said and done far off, until the enemy found the body, which his wife had betrayed, left at home deserted by its soul, and burnt it. Now this part is not true; the soul used not to go out from the body; but by always yielding to the

> spirit, and slackening the coupling bond, he gave it constant liberty to range around, so that it saw and heard and reported many things from the world outside. But those who destroyed the body while he was asleep are paying the penalty to this day in Tartarus. All this, young man, you shall know more clearly in the third month from this; now begone!" When the voice ceased, Timarchus wished to turn round, he said, and see who the speaker was; but his head again ached violently, as though forcibly compressed, and he could no longer hear or perceive anything passing about him; afterwards, however, he came to by degrees, and saw that he was lying in the cave of Trophonius, near the entrance where he had originally sunk down.
>
> 23. Such was the tale of Timarchus. When he died, having returned to Athens in the third month after hearing the voice ... (translation by de Lacy and Einarson, Loeb Library)

This account of the experiences of Timarchus in the cave of Trophonius is a unique document from the ancient world about a vision which has the quality of a "great dream." The vision, with its symbolism of disintegration and reintegration, bears all the marks of an initiation into the mystery of death. While it naturally contains much of the symbolism with which we have been dealing in connection with incubation rituals, it is at the same time a presentation of the ancient doctrine of the soul – a matter into which it is not possible to enter here. Cicero[38] says: "At multa falsa [scil. *somnii*]. Immo obscura fortasse nobis" ("but many of them [dreams] are deceptive; or perhaps rather unintelligible to us").

It will thus be seen that modern psychiatric shock treatment had its archetypal forerunners long before the discovery of insulin or of electricity, even though psychiatrists try nowadays to conceal the primitive character of this treatment under a clinical and scientific cloak. Psychologically, however, the ancient form

38 Cicero *De divin.* i. 29. 60.

of shock treatment was much more genuinely modern and more meaningful in that it laid special emphasis on the bringing of the shock experience into relation with consciousness.[39]

The correspondences between the primitive form of incubation ritual used in consulting Trophonius and the highly developed form in the cult of Asclepius are striking. It will be sufficient to draw attention to three features which are of particular interest to psychologists:

1. The *honey cakes* with which the serpents are fed were offerings which played a part in the cult of nearly all the chthonic deities. I need only mention the "earth-born ones," Cecrops and Erechtheus, who were also worshiped in the form of serpents and were given honey cakes of this kind. The sacred serpents in the Asclepieia were also fed with these cakes, a fact which shows that they represented chthonic aspects of Asclepius. We know from a mimiambus of Herondas[40] about Cos that the cakes in this form, when they were fed to the serpents, were called *popana* or *psaista,*[41] whereas after they had been consecrated and when they were burned on the altar, they were called *hygieia* or *mazia.*[42] This distinction corresponds exactly to that which we make between the unconsecrated *oblata* and the consecrated *hostia.*[43]

It would seem legitimate to draw up the following syllogism: Honey cakes were offerings made to the chthonii; the chthonii were prophetic; therefore, there is a link between honey and

39 Cf. p. 84.

40 Herondas iv. 90-95:

... place your offering
in the snake hole, quietly praying, and moisten
the sacrificial flour. The other we will eat
at our own hearth. And, hey, do not forget
to bring some of the blessed bread. He should give,
then you give him: when sacrificing, the blessed bread
is worth more than the loss of his share.

41 *Ibid.* iv. 92.

42 *Ibid.* iv. 94.

43 Cf. Richard Wünsch, "Ein Dankopfer an Asklepios," *Arch. Rel. Wiss.*, VII (1904), 95.

prophecy.[44] Support for this view can be found in Philostratus,[45] who speaks of the temple of Apollo at Delphi which was constructed of beeswax and feathers. This temple is also mentioned by Strabo[46] and Stobaeus.[47] An ancient Delphic oracle quoted by Plutarch[48] likewise refers to it. In this connection, it is noteworthy that the priestesses of Delphi were called bees, "Melissae."[49] The relation between honey and prophecy is particularly clear in the *Homeric Hymn to Hermes*.[50] This mentions three prophetic nymphs called "Thriae,"[51] who dwelt on Parnassus and who had taught Apollo the art of prophecy in his youth. These nymphs fed on honeycomb, and after eating it they spoke the truth. If they received no honey, they spoke lies. The association of honey and prophecy is also shown by the fact that the cave of Trophonius was discovered by Saon when he was following a swarm of bees.[52] The following dream will serve as an analogy:

XI. Scene: A forest lake of an incredibly dazzling blue. It is called "Ale Lake," ale of course meaning beer in English. In the middle there is a small island, made of a lump of resin or amber. There is a tall tree growing on it. There is a swarm of bees buzzing round the tree, and in the dream the bees are said to be caring for the tree as they fly round it.

2. The incubants were *prisoners of god*. In the rites of Trophonius the incubants were drawn down into the cave at such

44 Cf. also Ah. A. Lobeck, *Aglaophamus* (Königsberg, 1829), pp. 815 ff.
45 Philostratus *Vita Apoll. Tyan.* vi. II. 4.
46 Strabo ix. 421.
47 Stobaeus *Florileg.* xxi. 26.
48 Plutarch *De Pythiae orac.* 17: "Bring feathers, ye birds, and wax, ye bees."
49 Pindar *Pythian Odes* ii. 106 and Hesychius, *s.v.* Μέλισσαι; cf. also Porphyrius *De antr. nymph.* 8, as well as the fact that Deborah means "bee." Cf. W. Robert-Tornow, *De apium mellisque apud veteres significatione* (Berlin, 1893), pp. 30 ff.
50 *Homeric Hymn to Hermes* 552 ff.
51 The Greeks also used pebbles for divination, which were called *thriai*. Cf. Zenobius *Cent.* v and Stephanus of Byzantium, *s.v.* Θρία.
52 Pausanias ix. 40. 2. Cf. also Scholiast on Aristophanes *Clouds* 508.

time as he, in his divine wisdom, thought fit; they were sometimes kept there, whether they liked it or not, for several days without food or drink of any kind; and they were thrust out again when the god chose. I regard this fact as an important characteristic of the institution of incubation. It is alluded to in the worship of Asclepius only by the fact that patients sometimes had to wait until they had the right dream.[53] In the case of Serapis, the most celebrated of the colleagues of Asclepius and identified by many with him, we have definite information about the existence of the institution of *katochē*.[54] This means that the sick in search of healing – they were called *katochoi* – had to remain in the sacred precinct as prisoners of the god for perhaps a considerable time. Apuleius, too, called himself a *desmios* – a "bound captive" of the goddess Isis.[55]

The rhetorician Aelius Aristides (Aristides of Smyrna) tells us that the *enkatochoi* ("the imprisoned" or "the detained ones") made careful records of their dreams until a *symptōma,* that is, a coincidence with the dream of the priest, occurred.[56] Synchronicity and identity between the dreams of two persons seem to have been observed frequently and were always felt as having a healing effect.[57] An interesting parallel to this is to be found in

53 In earliest times, as I have already suggested, the first and only night was probably decisive. Miracle XXXIII (Herzog, *WHE*) is a case in point, where the patient, Thersandrus of Halieis, having had no dream, leaves the sanctuary the next morning. In Miracle XLVIII (*Ibid.*) the patient has to wait until the time ordained by the god has passed, and is then cured (τοῦ δὲ χρόνου παρελθόντος ὃ ποτετέτακτο). The orator Aeschines had to remain at the sanctuary for three months (*Ibid.*, Miracle LXXV), and a Demosthenes (*Ibid.*, Miracle LXIV) even four months. It seems, however, that these waiting periods prescribed by a dream only occur at a relatively late period.

54 Cf. R. Reitzenstein, *Die hellenistischen Mysterienreligionen* (Leipzig, 1927), Appendix III, and Erwin Preuschen, *Mönchtum und Sarapiskult* (Giessen, 1903).

55 Apuleius *Metam.* xi.

56 Aristides 473. 6 (ed. Dindorf). Cf. also *Oxyrhynchus Papyrus* XI.

57 Cf. Aristides ii, p. 401 (par. 30, ed. Keil), and Miracle XXII, Herzog, *WHE*. Note by the translator (Dr. Ethel Dorgan): An incident which shows that "coincidences" of this kind occur in modern psychotherapeutic practice happened to me while I was in the process of working on Chapter VII of this essay. One of my patients brought me a dream containing the following ...

the writings of Kant concerning Swedenborg.[58] Then, too, in Apuleius,[59] Isis says to Lucius in a dream:

> *Hoc eodem momento, quo tibi venio, simul et ibi praesens quae sunt sequentia praenuntio et sacerdoti meo per quietem facienda praecipio.*
>
> For in this same hour that I am come to thee, I am present there also and I command the priest by a vision what is to be done to bring about quietness.

For Apuleius, this *symptōma* is at the same time a sign that the time for consecration as a priest has come. Since he calls himself a priest of Asclepius,[60] we may assume that he had similar coincidental dreams at the sanctuary at Pergamum. This phenomenon is reminiscent of the incident in the Acts of the Apostles,[61] where the baptism of Cornelius, as well as that of Paul, requires sanction by a similar double dream.

With regard to the Asclepieium, Aristides says that the priest with whom he lodged outside the hieron frequently dreamed for him, and so did his own slave. He also emphasizes that it is worthwhile noting incidentals of the dream. The god recom-

passage: "I was going to a swimming bath which seemed to have two compartments. There was no water in the first compartment. I feared the second compartment, as I knew there was a great whirlpool to the right of it, and I felt myself being sucked into it. I felt helpless in the power of the suction, and said to two small men who were swimming-bath attendants that I wished I had known that the whirlpool was going to be there, as I would have taken more care not to be sucked into its power...." The remainder of the dream alludes unmistakably to the ideas of the *hieros gamos* and of rebirth. The imagery of the dream, especially the whirlpool and the "two small men," presents definite points of similarity with the account of the consultation of Trophonius. Dr. Meier feels that the dream deserves mention as "a living example of the phenomenon of the *symptōma* between the 'priest's' and patient's dreams."

58 Quoted from Lehmann-Petersen, *Aberglaube und Zauberei* (Stuttgart, 1925), III, 264-65.

59 Apuleius *Metam.* xi. 6 (trans. Adlington).

60 Apuleius *Florida* 18.

61 Cf. Acts of the Apostles 10.

mended him to do this from the outset and often actually dictated the text of the dream to him. He often wrote his speeches – he was an orator – "according to the voice of the god," *kata tas tōn oneiratōn epipnoias*. He then, as a matter of course, ascribed his success with the audience to the god – an excellent protection against the danger of inflation of the ego.

Asclepius often required a literary production of some kind as a thank offering – a paean, for example. Thus he became the patron of cultured and learned men and of artists. This is probably the chief reason why Plato[62] calls Asclepius the ancestor of the Athenians, and Tertullian[63] says the Athenians pay divine honors to Asclepius and his mother amongst their dead. We have already seen that the curative activity of the Asclepieia tended very definitely to the encouragement of the fine arts or, as Julian[64] says, the care of *sōma kai psychē* ("body and soul").

Apuleius formulated the fact of the *katochē* ("imprisonment" or "detention") in the mysteries of Isis with the admirable expression[65] *neque vocatus morari, nec non iussus festinare,* "[avoiding either that] if called upon I should delay, or not called should be hasty"; and the day of the summons – that is, his consecration as a priest – is to him *divino vadimonio destinatus,* the day "appointed when the sacrifice of dedication shall be done." Frequently a vision of unmistakable meaning was required as a sign for an applicant to be initiated into the mysteries. This corresponds to what in the cult of Asclepius is called "the effective or healing dream," which is the direct means of cure.[66]

The absolute authority attributed to decisions given by dreams is clear from Plato's *Republic*.[67] He says that Asclepius does not treat those who do not live a sound life, because they are of no

62 Plato *Symposium* 186 E.
63 Tertullian *Ad. nat.* ii. 14.
64 Julian *Contra Christ.* 235 B.
65 Apuleius *Metam.* xi. 21. 23 (trans. Adlington).
66 ἐνύπνιον ἐναργές ("effective dream"); cf. Libanius *De vita sua* 134.
67 Plato *Republic* iii. 14, 15 and 16.

use to the state. Philostratus[68] gives a fine example of this: Asclepius refuses to cure the patient because he is a drunkard and refers him to his mortal colleague, Apollonius of Tyana.[69] Another very striking incident is recorded in Iama (Cure) XXXVII from Epidaurus,[70] where the god tells a patient who is afraid of a cold bath that he will not cure men who are too cowardly to be cured. With regard to the conflict of competence between the doctor and the divine decree, especially as concerns the raising of the dead, consider the legend of Hippolytus, whom the mortal physician Asclepius raised from the dead with the result that he himself was punished with death.[71]

It can be clearly seen from the case of Aristides what an elegant solution can be found to transference problems when the doctor is not human but divine. Aristides was quite as much a "confirmed neurotic" as a famous rhetorician. He spent twelve years of his life, all told, in various Asclepieia, principally the one at Pergamum. He composed countless paeans *ad maiorem dei gloriam*,[72] which were sung all over Greece. Yet he did not have any serious inflated sense of importance, because he ascribed all his personal successes to the god. Even his choice of the profession of rhetorician was the work of Asclepius.[73] I have already mentioned the fact that Asclepius inspired poetry and song, and occasionally demanded such works of art in return as a reward.[74] Aristides regarded even his numerous illnesses as providential because they enabled him to make further progress in his intercourse with the god.[75]

68 Philostratus *Vita Apoll. Tyan.* i. 9.

69 On this subject cf. Hans Jenzer's study of Plato's 7th letter, in which the authority of the doctor and its ethical justification are discussed, and from which some remarkable philosophical considerations on the theme of euthanasia emerge. Hans Jenzer, *Das ärztliche Ethos im siebenten Brief Platos*; in *Sudhoffs Archiv*, 48 (1964), p. 17.

70 Herzog, *WHE*, pp. 24 f.

71 Cf. Vergil *Aeneid* vii. 765-73 and Lactantius Placidus *Comm. in Statium, ad Thebaidem* v. 434.

72 Aristides *Oratio* xxxviii.

73 *Ibid.* xxxxii. 13.

74 Cf. Suidas, *loc. cit.*

75 τῷ θεῷ συγγενόμενος, Aristides *Oratio* l, 26, 27.

I regard this conception as a classical prototype of that of the great doctor of the Romantic period, Christoph Wilhelm Hufeland. Hufeland has much to say in his *Makrobiotik,*[76] a work which is often unjustifiably depreciated, about the salutary effect of many intercurrent illnesses. The modern psychologist is often able to recognize the deeper significance of such complications when they arise in the course of psychological treatment.[77]

The "intercourse with the god" often has the character of a *unio mystica.* It is frequently with the god in his theriomorphic form. This applies quite literally in the case of women who consult Asclepius because they are barren; the god comes to them in the form of a serpent and impregnates them. Dreams of this kind are recorded on the Epidaurian stelae.[78] The technical terms were *syneinai* ("come together") or *henōsis* ("union"). This image is reminiscent of the *theos hypokolpios* ("lying in the lap"), as he was called in the mysteries; "the god in the form of a snake was drawn through under the garments of the initiate."[79] It need only be mentioned in passing that in the Christian forms of incubation the *synousia* with the god is very much clearer; indeed it develops into a regular symbolism of the *thalamos,* or bridal chamber.[80] I quote one example, concerning Bishop Basilius of Seleucia, from the *Life of St. Thecla:*[81]

> Everyone who had entered the sanctuary and said his prayer hastened at once to that cave and also, it is said, to some other sleeping place and bridal chamber, in which the virgin is to be found. Some say, too, that she is generally to be found in the latter chamber.

76 Christoph Wilhelm Hufeland, *Die Kunst, das menschliche Leben zu verlängern* (Jena, 1797).
77 Cf. Aristides *Oratio* xxiii. 16.
78 Herzog, *WHE,* Miracles XXXIX and XLII.
79 Cf. A. Dieterich, *Mithrasliturgie,* pp. 123 ff., and J.J. Bachofen, *Gräbersymbolik der Alten* (Basel, 1895), p. 152.
80 L. Deubner, *De Incubatione* (Leipzig, 1900), and Mary Hamilton, *Incubation* (London, 1906).
81 Deubner, *op. cit.,* p. 103.

This should be compared with what Irenaeus[82] says about the *thalamos* symbolism among the Marcosians. Bousset[83] calls the bridal chamber the most ancient sacrament. A particularly striking instance of this is to be found in Epiphanius: [84]

> ... so that they also dare to blaspheme concerning St. Elijah, and dare to maintain that he (Philippus) says that when he (Elijah) was carried up to heaven, he was thrown back again into the cosmos. For there came, so they say, a female demon who proved herself the stronger and asked him whither he was going. "For I have children by thee," she said "and (therefore) thou canst not rise up and leave thy children in the lurch." And he (Elijah) said, (Philippus relates), "How canst thou have children by me, for I lived chastely?" But she said, so they tell, "Nevertheless, when thou didst dream in thy sleep, thou didst often relieve thyself by an emission of semen. It was I that took the sperm from thee and bare thee sons" [*sōmata* = *spermata*].

In connection with this theme, compare the "green-clad woman" who meets Peer Gynt on his way with a loutish son whom he had had by her unconsciously.[85] Hippocrates[86] and Pliny[87] demonstrate that *synousia* represented a genuinely classical form of therapy.

The theme of the generation of outstanding men by divine or demonic serpents is widespread in the ancient world. According to Pausanias,[88] Asclepius in the form of a serpent becomes the father of Aratus. Alexander the Great was said to have been the son of a serpent, the god Ammon having had intercourse with

82 Irenaeus *Refut. omn. haer.* i. 21. 3.
83 W. Bousset, *Hauptprobleme der Gnosis* (Leipzig, 1907), p. 72, n. 2.
84 Epiphanius *Panarion* 26. 13. 4-5 (ed. Holl).
85 H. Ibsen, *Peer Gynt,* III. iii.
86 Hippocrates *Epid.* vi. 5, 15; vii. 123.
87 Pliny *Nat. Hist.* xxviii, 44 and 83.
88 Pausanias ii. 10. 3.

his mother Olympias in that form.[89] This legend of miraculous birth was later carried over to Augustus, who was regarded as a son of Apollo because the serpent which had intercourse with his mother, Atia, while she was sleeping in the temple of Apollo, was interpreted as being a form of that deity.[90] It will also be remembered in the story of Amor and Psyche by Apuleius that Psyche's sisters slander Eros, who comes by night, by saying that he is a serpent. The phallic aspect of the serpent naturally leads back to Panofka's Tychon, which I have already discussed above with regard to Telesphorus.

An interesting feature of the Epidaurian *iamata* is the treatment of poverty. Poverty in the ancient world had all the dignity of a sickness. *Nosos* and *penia,* "illness and poverty," belonged together in religious thought just as did *hygieia* and *ploutos,* "health and wealth," and were always cured at the same time. The identity of health and wealth in the ancient world is shown by Ariphron's *Hymn to Hygieia* and by Lycymnius;[91] that of illness and poverty by Leonidas of Tarentum,[92] Gaitulicus Lentulus,[93] and Cornelius Longus.[94] If a person was cured of poverty in the Asclepieium, it generally happened by means of a dream *oracle* which led to the discovery of a hidden treasure. Examples from Epidaurus are to be found in Miracles XLVI and LXIII.[95] This view is in irreconcilable opposition to the alchemical view, according to which poverty is an incurable sickness.[96]

Some of the detailed reports of cures which have come down to us prefigure the dialectical procedure of modern psychother-

89 Sidonius Apollinaris *Carmina* ii. 125-26.

90 Suetonius *Div. Aug. vita* 94. For other sons of serpents cf. Pausanias iv. 14. 7 f.

91 Lycymnius, Frag. 4, in Bergk-Hiller-Crusius, *Anthol. lyr.*, pp. 288-89.

92 Leonidas of Tarentum, *Palatine Anthology* vi. 300. 7 f.: "But if, as thou hast saved me from sickness so thou savest me from hateful penury, await a sacrifice of a kid" (trans. W.R. Paton).

93 Gaitulicus Lentulus, in *Ibid.* vi. 190. 9 f.: "But if, as thou hast driven away the disease that weighed sore on me, so thou dost drive away my poverty, I will give thee a fat goat" (trans. W.R. Paton).

94 Cornelius Longus, in *Ibid.* vi. 191. 4.

95 Herzog, *WHE.*

96 Yet even that can be cured by the panacea.

apy. These accounts often have a humorous flavor. Philostratus[97] relates that, when Asclepius forbade Polemon to drink cold water, he replied, *beltiste, ei boun epherapeues?* ("What would you have prescribed for an ox?"). When Asclepius commanded a certain Plutarchus to eat swine's flesh, the patient objected: "Lord, what would you have prescribed for a Jew?" Asclepius obligingly acquiesced in the witty objection of the Neo-Platonist and altered the treatment.[98] The dialectical character of the procedure is clearly shown in the consultation of the oracle of Faunus by King Latinus. Vergil[99] writes:

pellibus incubuit stratis somnosque petivit,
multa modis simulacra videt volitantia miris,
et varias audit voces fruiturque deorum
conloquio...

[The priest] lay on the spread-out skins and sought sleep. Many mysteriously flitting images passed before his eyes, and he heard manifold voices and took part in the conversation of the gods.

An authoritative method is used instead of a dialectical one in those cases where it was necessary to heal by means of paradoxes. This was always the case when a taboo had to be broken in order that a cure might be effected. This makes it clear that the primary consideration was the cure of the soul. At the same time it recalls the principle which has often been mentioned, that the poison, the forbidden thing, is at the same time the remedy. Examples of this are when a Syrian had to eat pork, a Jewess had to anoint her child with swine's fat, and a Greek woman, who was a devotee of Adonis, had to eat the flesh of a wild boar.

97 Philostratus *Vitae Sophist.* i. 25. 4.
98 Damascius, in Suidas, *s.v.* Δομνῖνος.
99 Vergil *Aeneid* vii. 88 ff.

Contraria contrariis.[100] Aristides[101] says: *kai mēn to ge paradoxon pleiston en tois iamasi tou theou* ("and it is in fact the paradox which is the highest thing in the god's cures").[102] Thus, for example, in the depth of winter Aristides is required amidst ice and snow to go down into the city and bathe in the river. "Still full of warmth from the sight of the god," he did so. For all the rest of the day he was filled with a sense of inexpressible well-being, so entirely was he "with the god." Only those who were among the initiated, *tōn tetelesmenōn esti,*[103] could understand or achieve this.

3. The symbolism of *death and birth* is even more striking in the rites of Trophonius than in those of Asclepius.[104] The process of being thrust in and out again through the hole is clearly a process of death and birth. The incubant is, as we have seen, dressed like an infant in swaddling clothes and afterwards is *quasimodo genitus;*[105] and it has already been pointed out in connection with the statue of Asclepius at Titane that the god himself there has the character of an infant in swaddling clothes and thus of an incubant. We possess statuettes of women initiated into the mysteries of Isis who are swaddled in this way.[106] What happened, therefore, was at the least a rebirth, *metagennēthēnai,* as in the mysteries of Mithras. Very often the incubants were fed on infant food, especially cheese, milk and honey.[107]

The dreams which follow are examples of the way in which these symbolical images and trains of events manifest themselves in the unconscious of modern man.

100 Cf. Weinreich, *AHW,* Appendix III.
101 Aristides *Oratio* xxxxii. 8.
102 Cf. also *Ibid.* xxxxvii. 47, 65.
103 Aristides *Hieroi logoi* 2, pars. 18-21 (ed. Keil, pp. 398 f.).
104 Cf. pp. 85 ff.
105 Pausanias x. 32. 16 and Frazer, *Pausanias,* V, 409.
106 Cf. Franz Cumont, *Die orientalischen Religionen im römischen Heidentum* (Leipzig and Berlin, 1931), Plate IV, illustration 4.
107 Cf. Apellas stele.

XII. I am going down a long flight of stairs carrying an infant whom I recognize as being myself wrapped in my mother's shawls.

Sometime later the same man had this dream:

XIII. I was running as fast as I could into a hill in which there were a great many tunnels; these were so deep and winding that I soon lost myself in them. The Devil was behind me all the time. I was sweating with fear and with the heat, which increased more and more, the further I penetrated into the *bowels* of the earth. At last I came to a deep cave, which was so far under the earth that I could feel the pressure of the earth, and the walls sweated with heat. At the end of a passage I looked down into a small round cave which had smooth walls; this showed that it was of *great age*. The walls were steel-blue, and yet glowing with heat. I was so full of fear and excitement that I covered my face with my arms. It was so quiet that I could hear the drops of sweat falling from my brow. In the center of the floor of the cave there lay a black human body, wrapped from head to foot in *linen bands* which looked as though they had been soaked in tar. The upper part of the body was propped up in a slanting position, as if on a dissecting table. The corpse was so dead that it looked as if it had lain countless ages in this tomb. All the same it was possible to recognize that this mummy – for that was what it looked like – had the face of a man. I recognized that *it was myself,* and I shivered in spite of the great heat, for I thought that now I was really *dead*. It now seemed to me that I myself passed into the corpse, and I struggled inside it against what seemed to hold me fast, but it was no use. I struggled again and again until at last something gave way. I made a still greater effort and something else gave way; I felt the bonds crack, and I struggled violently with all my strength, for I knew that I should die if I could not get free; I had the

> feeling that I should have to *give up the ghost*. I was filled with unimaginable terror. Then the corpse burst its bonds with a terrible cry, so that the *roof of the cave burst asunder,* and I saw the clear sky far above the roof. I left the corpse just as a bird takes wing and flies away, or as a *butterfly leaves its chrysalis,* and soared up into the dawn.

In most places where incubation was practiced, the incubants were strictly enjoined to wear white linen bands and white garments. There is no doubt that this garb also represents "putting on the new man." It is the outward and visible sign of transfiguration, and thus also the garment of the god, the indication of the "appearance of God."[108]

It will thus be seen that the incubant was changed from a *moriturus* into a *quasimodo genitus*. In view of all this, it is not surprising that the rite also healed people of bad fate or destiny.[109] Serapis, Asclepius' colleague, was often acclaimed with the phrase *panta nika ho Sarapis* ("Serapis overcomes all!"). This is strongly reminiscent of IĒSOUS CHRISTOS NIKA ("Jesus Christ conquers").

This also throws light on the fact that Serapis only abandoned the function of healing as late as A.D. 391, when his temple in Alexandria was destroyed by the fanatical bishop Theophilus. Asclepius, like Serapis, was specially detested by the early Christian bishops. Certainly few ancient temples were destroyed with such persistent zeal as were those of Asclepius.[110] The many parallels between Asclepius and Christ explain this zeal. The extensive polemical writings of the Early Fathers provide ample evidence. Yet, within the world of late pagan antiquity, Asclepius achieved the highest divine rank, as can be seen from Aristides;[111] and he actually gives the god the status of the Pla-

108 μορφὴ θεοῦ
109 κακὴ συναστρία (*constellatio*) or κακὴ εἱμαρμένη
110 Cf. Eusebius Caesariensis *De vita Constantini* iii. 56 and Sozomenus *Hist. eccl.* ii. 5.
111 Aristides *Oratio* xxxxii. 4.

tonic world soul.[112] Asclepius healed without asking anything in return. He did not even demand that the person who asked for his help should believe in him, but only that he should be a decent man. He was free from resentment or revengefulness, and his miracles occurred in and through the closest personal contact between him and the invalid. The *sōtēr kat' exochēn* ("savior par excellence"), as Thrämer[113] calls him, became the strongest rival of Christ next to Mithras.[114] The Fathers regarded him as a prefiguration of Christ contrived by the Devil. The heathen said: "The miraculous cures which Jesus performs, he performs in the name of Asclepius."[115] The name Jesus was often derived, though wrongly (even by Eusebius[116]), from Asclepius' daughter Iaso and the verb *iasthai,* "to heal." Julianus,[117] speaking of the philanthropic spirit of the god, says:

> *Oude gar ho Asklēpios ep' amoibēs elpidi tous anthrōpous iatai, alla to oikeion autǭ philanthrōteuma pantaxou plēroi.*
>
> For Asclepius does not heal in the expectation of reward, but manifests everywhere the benevolent disposition which is characteristic of him.

In this respect Asclepius is a successor to Hermes, who was once called the god most friendly to men.[118] It is important that the ancients, in speaking of the cures which modern rationalism calls miraculous (using the word as a synonym for priestly deceit or charlatanism) never used the expression *thaumata* ("wonders"). This is to be found exclusively in Christian writings. The

112 *Ibid.* xxxxx. 56.
113 E. Thrämer in P.-W., *s.v.* "Asklepios."
114 It is interesting to remember in this connection that Mithras, the god of mysteries, is accompanied by dog and snake just like Asclepius.
115 Justinus *Apol.* 54. 10.
116 Cf. A. Harnack, *Medizinisches aus der ältesten Kirchengeschichte* (1892), pp. 89 ff., and *Dogmengeschichte* (Tübingen, 1909), I^4, 136, 165.
117 Julianus *Epistulae* 78. 419 B.
118 Kern, *Religion,* II, 19.

ancient Greek term is *aretai* or *epiphaneiai*. *Aretē* here means goodness or an outstanding deed performed on the basis of a *dynamis* ("power"), which corresponds to the primitive conception of mana or orenda. For this reason the most natural occurrences can also be *aretai*.

CHAPTER VIII

THE MYSTERY OF HEALING

MORE THAN ONCE I have intimated in the preceding pages that incubation had the character of a mystery. This was shown in rather more detail in the passages dealing with the summons to incubation and the nocturnal character of the healing ritual. As we have seen, the postulant in the mysteries was summoned to initiation by dreams. In other respects, too, the idea of the mystery can be perceived as an underlying factor in the ritual of incubation. I should like to give further evidence of this. One of the most important points is what has already been said about birth symbolism. The incubant was reborn, healed, after a visit to the underworld. Surely this is the same thing as what Apuleius tells us about the mysteries of Isis. Moreover, when the postulant emerged from the mysteries, he was himself a *religiosus,* a *cultor deae:* this corresponds to the Greek term *therapeutēs,* which was dealt with at the beginning of this essay. Then, too, when Aristides[1] unhesitatingly entitled his "case history" – which runs to some 30,000 lines – *Hieroi logoi,* he was saying quite simply that he regarded it as a mystery; for this expression was a technical term for the mystery myths.[2]

Mysteries presuppose *epoptai* (spectators), who see the *drōmenon* (action). In the case of incubation, the incubant would have been the *epoptēs,* and the *drōmenon* which he had witnessed would have been the dream; while the healing itself would have been the mystery. Aristides[3] several times explicitly calls Asclepius' cures "mysteries."

Such mysteries are of course personal in the most intimate

1 Aristides *Oratio* xxxxviii. 3.
2 *Ibid.* xxxxii. 4 and 11.
3 *Ibid.* xxiii. 16.

sense. The words of Reitzenstein[4] apply here: "The initiate in the mysteries does not merely witness what the god experiences; he experiences it himself, and thus becomes the god...." In any case he was *monos pros monon,* alone with the god, and could converse with him; there was a real dialectical situation, and a personal mystery of this kind led to *gnōsis theou* ("knowing God"). The ideas of mystery and healing agree, too, in the fact that the transformation was a *timē* ("distinction"), which was often granted without anything being done to deserve it. I should like to give further proof of this.

As already mentioned, Tacitus reports that a Eumolpid, a priest of the Eleusinian mysteries, played an important part in the founding of the first Serapeum. One of the inscriptions at Epidaurus[5] mentions a "hierophant," which was the technical term for an initiating priest of Eleusis.[6] Aristides says that Asclepius bade him always sacrifice to the Eleusinian goddesses as well as to Asclepius himself, and the Apellas stele says the same.[7] The Orphic *Hymn to Hygieia* contains the lines:

> Come then, blessed goddess,
> To the seekers of *mystic* healing.

Demeter *phōsphoros,* "light-bringer," as a healing goddess accompanied by serpents was worshiped in the Asclepieium at Pergamum. A statue of Asclepius with Hygieia adorned the entrance to the temple of Demeter-Cora at Megalopolis.[8] The equation of Asclepius with the deities of the Eleusinian mysteries can also be deduced from Minucius Felix.[9] The fact that Demeter at Eleusis was likewise a goddess of healing is shown by a votive relief of Eurates, offered in thanks for the cure of an eye

4 R. Reitzenstein, *Die hellenistischen Mysterienreligionen* (Leipzig, 1927), Appendix III, p. 22.
5 *IG,* IV^2, 1, No. 438.
6 *IG,* I^2, 3, 76, 24.
7 Herzog, *WHE,* pp. 43 f.
8 Pausanias viii. 31. 1.
9 Minucius Felix *Octavius* vi. 1.

disease (this also conveys the idea of making conscious, i.e., "seeing" intellectually),[10] as well as by an epigram of Antiphilus.[11] Other examples are given by Frazer.[12] At Cos, too, there was a cult of Demeter, as is shown by Stelae 8 and 17.[13]

On the 17th Boedromion – a day of the Greater Eleusinian Mysteries – a festival was celebrated in the temple of Asclepius at Athens to commemorate the initiation of Asclepius into the Eleusinian mysteries. Pausanias[14] writes:

> The Athenians say that they initiated Asclepius into their mysteries on that day, which is therefore called Epidauria (*ta Epidauria*), and that since that time they paid divine honors to him.

This took place at first in the temple of the Eleusinian goddesses, and the festival began with a *pannychis*[15] (night festival), emphasizing its nocturnal character. The *kanēphoroi* (maidens who carried baskets at processions) and the *arrēphoroi* (maidens who carried the symbols of Athena) walked in procession with the *cista mystica* ("mystic basket").[16] Philostratus[17] says in his description of the Eleusinian mysteries:

> It was the day of the Epidauria. On this day the Athenians were accustomed to carry out initiations after the predictions [*prorrhēseis*[18]] and the festivals [*hiereia*]. This was instituted on account of Asclepius, because they had initiated him in his lifetime, when he came from Epidaurus,

10 *Ephem. archaiol.* (1892), pp. 113 ff., Plate V, quoted from Kern, *Religion*, II, 205.
11 Antiphilus, *Palatine Anthology* ix. 298.
12 J.G. Frazer, *Pausanias*, V, 619.
13 R. Herzog, "Heilige Gesetze von Kos."
14 Pausanias ii. 26. 8.
15 Aristides *Oratio* xxxxvii. 6.
16 *IG*, II^2, No. 974.
17 Philostratus *Vita Apollon. Tyan.* iv. 18.
18 Cf. the deacon's exhortation after the mass of the catechumens that all those not yet baptized should leave.

although the celebration of the mysteries had already reached an advanced stage.

After this glorious reception given to Asclepius in Athens, we should not be surprised to find that his temple existed there as late as the fifth century A.D.[19]

I hope that the material brought together in this study does more than explain the laconic dream about Epidaurus quoted at the beginning. I believe, too, that the amplifications which have been added illustrate how much the experiences and methods of modern psychotherapy correspond to the methods and the conceptions underlying healing in classical times. The psyche, the most subjective part of man, is revealed here as faithful to its own timeless laws and to the *consensus omnium. Nomina mutantur, permanent numina:* time may effect changes of viewpoint, but, though the *nomina* change, the *numina* and their effects remain ever the same.

19 Marinus *Vita Procli* 29.

EPILOGUE

THE DREAM IN ANCIENT GREECE

I.

How the dream was viewed in ancient Greece has a long history: at the beginning, as far as we know, the attitude was purely religious, whereas in the end the dream had become a prey to cheap impostors found by the dozen in every market-place, at every festival or country fair. Incidentally, the extreme diversity of significance accorded the dream is manifest in many other cultures, so that it might almost appear to be either a cultural pattern or the result of something inherent in the phenomenon of the dream itself. But the wide variety of meanings attributed to dreams has not only been a function of the dreamer's lifetime but also demonstrably of his social standing, education, or philosophy. And here the correlation may have been direct or inverse, just as it is in our day. If we try to find a *constant,* it consists most probably in the dreamer's attitude toward the *irrational*. Interestingly enough, one phenomenon connected with dreams has survived the tides of changing opinion for several thousand years; incubation was practiced in the most archaic caves, for example, of Amphiaraus at Oropus or Trophonius at Lebadea, and is still flourishing at many Christian shrines today, and not only in Greece.[1] I point out later some of the reasons for this striking fact.

Here I select, in chronological order, some of the more important things that Greek poets, philosophers and medical men had to say about the dream.

In Homer *oneiros* is always a personified and at the same time divine (*theios*) and winged being that appears to the dreamer

1 Mary Hamilton, *Incubation* (London, 1906).

hyper kephalēs (at the head of his bed) and disappears again, being independent of time and space. Nestor, for instance, visiting Agamemnon in a dream, calls himself *Dios de toi angelos eimi*[2] ("I am a messenger of Zeus"), and his task is to tell Agamemnon the will of God. This example may be taken as a model for almost all Homeric dreams, and they all come from Zeus. In the so-called *Homeric Hymn to Hermes* this god is called the *hēgētōr oneirōn,* the guide or mediator of dreams. It certainly strikes us as significant that the gods, as a rule, appear in person and speak directly to the dreamer (*quod ipsi dii cum dormientibus colloquantur*).[3] From innumerable dreams related in ancient literature it is apparent that everybody was convinced that dreams were messages from the gods. More theoretically, and theologically or philosophically, this may be explained by the Orphic idea of *sōma-sēma* (which we find again in Plato's *Phaedrus* 250 C), since in sleep the soul is freed from its tomb (the body) whereby it is sensitized and so is able to perceive and converse with higher beings, a thought that was also held by the Pythagoreans. This idea can be found in Aeschylus and Euripides still, as well as in Pindar[4] and Xenophon.[5] It goes without saying that dreams of such dignity must be carefully observed and interpreted, an attitude that is reflected in Aeschylus' *Prometheus Bound,* where it is said that dream interpretation is one of the most important inventions of Prometheus.[6] The high dignity of dreams also made it imperative to go to any length in order to avert the evil that, according to the dream, was impending. Either such a dream had to be told to Helios, whose bright daylight would frighten away its dangerous implications,[7]

2 Homer *Iliad* ii. 26.
3 Cicero *De divinatione* i. 64; Homer, *Iliad* x. 496; *Odyssey* xvi. 21-24; xx. 32.
4 Pindar, *Frag.* 131 S.
5 Xenophon *Cyropaedia* viii. 7. 21.
6 Aeschylus *Prometheus Bound* 486.
7 Sophocles *Electra* 424 and scholia; Euripides, *Iphigenia in Tauris* 42.

or sacrifices had to be made to the apotropaic gods.[8] In minor cases lustration with water seems to have been sufficient.[9] In Euripides we find another interesting aspect of dreams when he calls Lady Earth (*potnia Chthōn*) "Mother of black-winged Dreams" (*melanopterygōn mēter oneirōn*).[10] It is this chthonic origin of dreams which has survived down to our time in the practice of incubation. More about this presently.

Plato did not create a theory of dreams except that in his psychology it becomes clear that the content of a dream is determined by the particular part of the psyche that is active, namely the *logistikon,* the *thēriōdēs,* or the *thymoeidēs*. If the *logistikon* prevails, however, we may have a dream that reveals to us the all-important truth.[11] In regard to such dreams, Xenophon, in his *Commentary,* clearly advocates interpretation, as ordinary knowledge may not suffice for their understanding. In the *Symposium,*[12] moreover, Plato calls a man who knows how to judge dreams a *daimonios anēr* as opposed to the *banausos*. But these are the words of Diotima, his specialist on Eros, and according to her, demons are the originators of dreams and oracles, and one of these demons is Eros. It should be noted that Plato attributes this view to a woman.

We deal briefly now with the most powerful authority on dreams, Aristotle. Two opuscula contained in the *Parva Naturalia* are in relatively good condition: (1) "On the Dream" and (2) "On Prophecy in Sleep" (especially 464*b*). According to these, the dream is the result of the affection of the *koinon aisthētērion,* that is, the heart as the central seat of representations, by those minimal movements during sleep left over from the waking activities of the senses. These residual movements are, of course, present

8 Xenophon *Symposium* iv. 33; Hippocrates, *Peri enypniōn* ii. 10 (ed. D.C.G. Kühn [Lipsiae, 1826]).

9 Aeschylus *Persians* 200; Aristophanes *Frogs* 1339; Apollonius Rhodius *Argonautica* iv. 662; for further examples, see B. Büchsenschütz, *Traum und Traumdeutung im Alterthume* (Berlin, 1868).

10 Euripides *Hecuba* 70.

11 Plato *Republic* ix. 571 C ff.

12 Plato *Symposium* 203 A.

in the waking state, too, but remain unperceived – unheard, as it were – because of the violent movements of the senses, that is, because of the far greater noise they make. This is how veridical dreams are possible, because during sleep the dreamer is much more sensitive to small disturbances of an organic nature. A skilled doctor can therefore predict illness, cure, or death from such dreams.

Dreams about people we know well can, according to Aristotle, also be veridical or precognitive, because we know these people's motivations well and are consciously deeply involved with them, so that from such knowledge we can reach certain conclusions concerning their future actions.

Also, according to Aristotle, the dream is an incentive to future actions of the dreamer. Concerning the diagnostic and prognostic use of dreams, Aristotle closes his treatise "On Prophecy in Sleep" with an interesting simile by which he shows how dreams can and should be understood and interpreted:

> The most skilful judge of dreams is the man who possesses the ability to detect likenesses; for anyone can judge the vivid dream. By likenesses I mean that the mental pictures are like reflections in water, as we have said before. In the latter case, if there is such movement, the reflection is not like the original, nor the images like the real object. Thus *he* would indeed be a clever interpreter of reflections who could quickly discriminate, and envisage these scattered and distorted fragments of the images as representing a man, say, or a horse or any other object. Now in the other case too the dream has a somewhat similar result; for the movement destroys the clarity of the dream.[13]

Generally speaking, Aristotle paradoxically sides with Diotima when he attributes a *demonic* origin to dreams. Were they

13 Aristotle, "On Prophecy in Sleep" in *Parva Naturalia,* from W.S. Hett, trans., *On the Soul; Parva Naturalia, On Breath* (Cambridge, Mass.: Harvard University Press, 1936), p. 385.

sent by God, he argues, they would only be bestowed on the best and wisest men, which is most obviously not so. This sweeping devaluation of the dream has had a lasting effect in the West. For example, the Epicureans, as well as the New Academy philosophers like Carneades, naturally had as little use for dreams as did the Cynics. But in the Stoa, dreams again play a prominent part. The ancient Stoics seem to have been the first to classify dreams[14] by their sources: they come either from God or from demons or from the activity of the soul itself. Apart from this, the Stoics allow for prognostication through dreams by virtue of the interrelation of the human soul with the soul of the universe. Because of these correspondences man is aware of the coherence of all things when his senses are at rest – that is, in his sleep – and thus he is able to know the future.[15] Poseidonius[16] claims that the *divine* has three ways of acting upon man in dreams: (1) the soul may see the future by virtue of its own god-like nature; (2) the air is full of immortal souls carrying obvious signs of truth, who penetrate the sleeper's system through the channels (*poroi*) of the senses;[17] and (3) the gods themselves talk to the sleepers.[18]

These thoughts, together with the idea of the macrocosm-microcosm relation, seem to give almost a causal explanation for all mantic belief: the order of the universe consists of the concatenation of causes and effects. Certain signs let us perceive certain causes that will lead to certain effects. In turn, these signs are perceived in certain dreams: "Poseidonius esse censet in natura signa quadam rerum futurarum."[19]

This theory, in my opinion, certainly allows for precognitive or veridical dreams, or rather dreams to be so interpreted,

14 *Stoicorum Veterum Fragmenta* iii. 605.
15 *Ibid.* ii. 1198.
16 Cicero *De divin.* i. 30.
17 Plutarch *De placitis philosophorum* v. 2; *Quaestiones conviviales* viii. 10. 2.
18 Karl Reinhardt, *Poseidonios über Ursprung und Entartung* (Heidelberg: Carl Winters Universitätsbuchhandlung, 1928), pp. 457-459.
19 Cicero *De divin.* i. 52-57.

whereas for the possibility of so-called telepathic dreams one must resort to a theory that had already been proposed by Democritus, astonishingly enough. His atoms or *eidōla* have all the qualities of an *individuum,* the Latin word created by Cicero in translating the Greek *hē atomos* (the atom) of Democritus. The air is full of atoms-individuals that offer themselves as carriers of messages from one person to another, which should indeed make it easy to transmit telepathic effects.[20] As I have already committed an anachronism by going back to Democritus, let me do so again by calling your attention to the well-known Fragment 89 D of Heraclitus: *tois egrēgorosin hena kai koinon kosmon einai, tōn de koimōmenōn hekaston eis idion apostrephesthai* ("the waking have one world and a common one, but when asleep everyone turns away from it into his own world"). His *own world* therefore must be his dreamworld, where he is all by himself, in a primordial condition; in other words, the dreamer finds himself in a mythological realm and what happens there is actually cosmogony. In this sense Heraclitus' saying corresponds exactly with Jung's concept of the meaning of dreams "on the subjective level."

Now to outline the medical approach to dreams in Greece, we go back to the fifth century B.C. where we find a Hippocratic writer dealing with the problem in *Peri enypniōn.*[21] According to this treatise, the soul is preoccupied with bodily functions during the waking state, whereas in sleep she is the unrestricted ruler of the house, since the sleeping body has no perception. While the body sleeps, the soul, which is always awake, has all the psychological and physiological functions at her disposal, so that he who is able to judge this relationship correctly possesses a good deal of wisdom. Hippocrates also admits that there can be divine influences in dreams through which we can know things otherwise unknowable. Regarding the diagnostic value of dreams, he thinks the soul can perceive the causes of illness in *images* dur-

20 *Ibid.* i. 43; ii. 67.
21 Pseudo-Hippocrates *Peri enypniōn* ii. 1-16.

ing sleep. Here we see for the first time that a symbolic quality of the psyche is assumed. When Hippocrates is particularly interested in the medical aspect, he shows very clearly that the health of the dreamer is reflected in his dream. There are, of course, *divinely* inspired dreams, interpretation of which he leaves entirely to the dream specialist. But then there are the *natural* influences whereby the soul perceives the bodily condition and thus becomes a hygienic system, which functions in the following way: as long as the dream simply repeats what has happened during the day, the body is obviously in order. But when the dream pictures strife, war and the like, this means disorder in the body. When we, for instance, dream of the sun and the moon as they appear in nature, this is a sign of good health, but when something is wrong with these planets in our dream, then there must be something the matter with those systems in us which correspond to sun and moon according to the macrocosm-microcosm relation. Springs and wells correspond to the uropoietic system, rivers to the circulatory system where flood or drought would be the same, for example, as hypertonia or anemia.[22] Galen had little more to say about this problem. The diagnosis, as the examples have shown, was reached exclusively from the dream text by what we might call "thinking in analogies." And this technique has been called by several authors the only significant point in the art of dream interpretation.[23]

It is evident that there is hardly anything new in the dream theories of Hippocrates and Galen as compared with those of Plato, Aristotle and Democritus. Plato and Aristotle already had the idea that dreams stemmed from the perception of residual movements in sleep. Those inner movements are the dream images that are exclusively based on an inner faculty of perception – *phantasia.* Aristotle's psychology could be called a differential computation of the mutual inhibitions, stimulations, overlays, and interferences of those inner movements. But medical

22 Hippocrates *Peri diaitēs* iv. 88 ff. (English trans. W.H.S. Jones [London and New York, 1931], IV, 421-447).
23 Aristotle, "On Prophecy in Sleep" 464^b 5; Artemidorus *Oneirocritica* ii. 25.

men could apply this dream theory to therapy only by cutting out all extraneous sources for dreams. The *somnia a deo missa* had to be excluded. And here we touch upon a decisive distinction regarding the immanence or transcendence of the source. Medical and rationalistic influence became very strong and almost replaced the purely religious attitude of the earlier days. It is clear that the transcendent source had been the only one that interested the Greek peoples earlier. Dreams were considered to be objective facts, things that happened to you. The Greek was "visited" by a dream (*episkopein*), at best he "saw" a dream (*enypnion idein*). They would never have dreamed of saying as the French do nowadays, "J'ai fait un rêve," or the Italians, "Ho fatto un sogno." We could therefore predict that after this rationalistic period the pendulum would swing again in the other direction. We have but to look at the Hellenistic period of which I take Philo as an example. To him the most important organ is the *pneuma*. It is the *psychē psychēs,* the soul of the soul, that has the cleanest and best *ousia,* substance, namely a divine one. The dream is to him a phenomenon in which the pneuma is the protagonist. Therefore all dreams are interesting mainly for their prophetic quality. Philo has three categories of dreams: (1) dreams prophetic by direct divine influence; (2) dreams prophetic by virtue of the movement of the *ratio* inasmuch as it is in harmony with the general divine movement; and (3) dreams that spring from purely psychic emotions because of the powers of enthusiasm. Only dreams in the last category need interpretation, though here, too, the enthusiastic powers point to divine origin, and generally speaking *all* is irrational again. This trend prevailed to Roman times.

This lopsided enthusiastic view is of course as unsavory as the purely rationalistic one. The early Homeric distinction should never be forgotten.[24] There will always be confused, relatively unimportant dreams that penetrate the Gate of Ivory, and clear and very significant dreams that come through the Gate of Horn.

24 Homer *Odyssey* xix. 560 ff.

(Penelope's dream of the geese and the eagle, by the way, is interpreted purely allegorically and not symbolically in Jung's terminology.) It is rather on the strength of such a dichotomy that dreams can be taken seriously at all, as is shown very impressively by Greek dreamers who had temples built, sacrifices performed, and so on, because of dreams.[25]

I am strongly disposed to believe that almost all the observations of the Greeks on dreams still hold good. There are a few obvious exceptions owing to changes in cultural conditions: for instance, with everything so utterly secularized with us, there are rarely any divine epiphanies in our dreams. And, for the same reason, it is no longer true nowadays that only kings, priests or medical men have dreams of great import.

So far the scanty sources about dreams in ancient literature have had to be carefully and painstakingly collected, a task carried out mainly by B. Büchsenschütz[26] and to some extent by E.R. Dodds.[27] Unfortunately all the important books on dreams written in antiquity have been lost, and for synopses of them we must look to authors of the second and fourth centuries A.D., namely Artemidorus (who calls himself "of Daldis," although he was born in Ephesus), and Macrobius and Synesius of Cyrene. Artemidorus has the advantage of having known all the antique literature on dreams as well as having been in practice for a lifetime. He not only collected more than three thousand dreams, but also took a good look at the dreamers themselves and correlated their life histories with their dreams in order to evaluate the dreams' eventual significance. This proves beyond a doubt that he had scientific interests, a point I wish to emphasize because he is usually taken much less seriously than he should be. The reasons for the prejudice that he meets with among us would be worthy of a careful psychological analysis. Compared to Artemidorus, Macrobius and Synesius were highly educated men who reflected on dreams more independently and were much less

25 Aelius Aristides (A.D. 117 or 129-189).
26 Büchsenschütz, *op. cit.*
27 E.R. Dodds, *The Greeks and the Irrational* (Berkeley and Los Angeles, 1956).

influenced by the earlier dream literature; but they were philosophical scholars rather than practitioners. Macrobius was an initiate in the Neo-Platonic mysteries, and Synesius became a Christian bishop (with wife and children!) though he had never been baptized, a fact that testifies to his scholarly merits and prestige. He had to be won over to Christianity at all costs, but proved reluctant to accept the episcopacy unless he "was allowed to philosophize at home and mythologize in church." Contrary to Artemidorus, who is an eclectic, Macrobius and Synesius, who may be counted as the first Neo-Platonists to have been baptized, are both true to their Neo-Platonic convictions. Briefly, Synesius maintains that his book *Peri enypniōn* was written in one night, at God's command. With him dreams are prophetic inasmuch as through and in them we practice what will, according to cosmic harmony, happen to us later anyhow. They are the preludes to the events and they may tune us into them. They are the best kind of prophecy because they come to all men, poor and rich. Dreams arise from the soul, which contains the images of things to come. These images are reflected in "phantasy," which is a kind of life on a deeper level. Its sense organs are finer, more divine, hence more reliable than ours, but its perceptions are blurred, which is a wise limitation and accounts for the need for interpretation. Synesius gives no general rule for interpretation but strongly recommends that we keep "nightbooks" instead of silly diaries. Macrobius' "Commentariorum ex Cicerone in Somnium Scipionis libri duo"[28] first gives a classification of dreams closely resembling that of Artemidorus. Then it supplies a long and exhaustive context to Scipio's dream text and goes to great lengths to provide exactly what we would today call an amplification of the material according to C.G. Jung. In this way we learn that the dreamer by means of his dream was not only given a thorough lecture on contemporary psychology but was truly initiated into the mysteries of his soul, an initiation that winds up with the mystagogue's assertion "deum te esse scito."

28 In Cicero *De republica* vi.

Toward the end of the book, Macrobius also presents a very useful and reliable synopsis of most of the Greek philosophers' ideas about the nature of the psyche. Macrobius' interesting classification has been available since 1952 in a good annotated English translation.[29]

I would like to point out some of the more unusual qualities of Artemidorus' five books of *Oneirocritica,* because his views give us a chance to compare ancient ideas with modern ones. I will skip over his classification, which as you already know is in Macrobius in translation, but keep in mind that he scrutinized three thousand dreams and carefully investigated the dreamers' personal circumstances as well as the outcome (anamnesis, catamnesis and epicrisis).

(1) What stands out as important is the fact that in contradistinction to modern dream material a large proportion of his dreams contain divine epiphanies. Here he knows of one and only one absolutely reliable criterion, that is, (2) as long as the god appears true to his attributes and to his cult-image, the dream is favorably interpreted. The slightest flaw in this respect, however, renders its meaning ominous. This conviction clearly reveals a totemistic element. With aborigines of northwestern Australia, odd behavior of the totem animal in dreams is always interpreted unfavorably (personal communication from Rix Weaver, Perth, W. Australia). Gods appearing in a wrong costume may easily lie. It seems that such deviations had the quality of blasphemy, which psychologically meant that the dreamer was in conflict with whatever deeper psychological truth or quality the particular god represented. This would of necessity call down the god's wrath upon the dreamer. Generally speaking we notice here the common features of ancient *oneiromanteia,* namely, that all dreams are mainly judged (3) in terms of future actual events and (4) as to whether they will turn out favorably or unfavor-

29 W.H. Stahl, *Macrobius' Commentary on the Dream of Scipio* (New York: Columbia University Press, 1952). An edition of this text by M. Nisard and with a French translation is included in the "Collection des Auteurs Latins" (Paris, 1883).

ably. (5) The particular dreamer's god also has to obey the rule of *suum cuique,* so that goddesses, for instance, are considered more appropriate for women than for men. (6) Gods may appear only as their attributes (*pars pro toto*), which is another reason why the interpreter (as well as for [2]) had to be very well informed in mythology (trees and so forth). (7) Gods may make prescriptions, even in the medical sense, in the event of physical illness. These prescriptions are very simple and need no interpretation. A god speaks in riddles only in order to make us ponder the dream (IV.22). (8) There are two kinds of dreams: (*a*) *theorēmatikoi* and (*b*) *allēgorikoi*. The dreams in group (*a*) correspond exactly to reality and very soon after being dreamed are *tale quale* lived out by the dreamer. The dreams in group (*b*) have a deeper meaning, shown *di' ainigmata* ("through enigmas"), and take a long time to come true, sometimes years. (9) There are dreams that come from within and dreams that come from without. All dreams containing unexpected elements belong to the latter category since they are regarded as being sent by the gods (*theopempton*).

Concerning these principles of interpretation, I will point out a few peculiarities that compare favorably with modern principles. (1) There are relatively few standard equations for typical dream elements, as for instance:

business = mother, because it is nurturing
business = wife, because of the close connection between a man and his business
head = father
foot = slave
right hand = father, son, friend, brother
left hand = wife, mother, mistress, daughter, sister
pudendum = parents, wife, children

(2) There are six *stoicheia* (elements) to be found in all dreams: nature, law, custom, professional skill, art and name. Everything in the dream that takes its course in harmony with its

nature, law, and the rest, is of good omen; what deviates in one way or another is of bad omen. (3) You must know all about the dreamer's life (anamnesis) and situation; if necessary you must seek information from others (objective anamnesis). (4) You must know the dreamer's character. (5) You must consider the dreamer's actual mood. (6) You must be given the whole dream; fragments must not be interpreted (IV.3). (7) You must be familiar with the customs of the place and of the people in order to judge the dream correctly according to (2). (8) Etymology should always be used, particularly in the case of proper names. (Thus a Greek dreaming of a Eutychos, or a Roman of a Felix, should take this as a good sign because both names mean literally "happy.")

(9) We will now dwell a bit on the most prominent feature of Artemidorus' approach, the *polarity* and *ambivalence* of dream motives, of which I give some examples:

a) To have asses' ears is a good omen only for a philosopher because the ass will not listen and give in easily. To all other people it means servitude and misery (I.24).

b) Taking a bath: formerly this was performed after tedious work and would consequently have indicated sweat and tears. Nowadays it is a sign of wealth and luxury and consequently a good omen (I.64).

c) To sleep in the temple indicates a cure to the sick, illness to the healthy (I.79).

d) Gold as such is of good omen, but should a man, for instance, wear a gold necklace it would be the opposite (II.5).

e) Being struck by a flash of lightning takes from you what you possess. As the poor possess poverty and the rich wealth, the portent of such a dream is accordingly good or bad (II.9).

f) A dolphin *in* water is of good omen, *out of* water of bad omen (II.16).

g) Something bad happening to your enemies is of good omen to you (I.2).

h) If you are happy and are promised happiness in the dream, this means bad luck; if you are unhappy, good luck. Conversely, should you be unhappy and dream that you will be unhappy, it means good luck.

i) Simple people dream directly, whereas people who know a lot about dreaming in their dreams translate the crude facts into symbols (IV. Introduction). This is in the genuine Sophoclean tradition: "For wise men author of dark edicts aye, / For dull men a poor teacher, if concise."[30] Generally speaking, people have pleasant dreams when they live under unpleasant conditions. Explaining this ambivalence or multivalence of dream "symbols," Artemidorus simply points out that the facts in life *are* ambivalent.

j) In IV.67 he gives a striking paradigm for seven different meanings of an identical dream dreamed by seven different pregnant women: all dreamed that they had given birth to a dragon. The interpretation had to be adapted to the particular circumstances of the dreamer's life, her anamnesis, for in each case the *apobasis* ("ending") was actually different.

k) Artemidorus makes allowance for wish fulfillment in dreams by saying that we want the god to help us to see more clearly what is going on in us. In this sense we are disposed to ask what, in fact, our dreams are. But, he adds, we should never ask the gods undue questions either! And if the answer has been granted, we must not forget to sacrifice and give thanks (IV.2).

l) In the art of dream interpretation you must skillfully synthesize all these and many more principles and never forget *respicere finem,* to adapt your verdict to the personality of the dreamer before you (III.66). Many a dream must remain uninterpreted until its *apobasis* is known (IV.24).

m) In IV.20 we find advice for the scribes among analysts. He says in so many words that the analyst should, after due consideration of all the circumstances mentioned above, present his interpretation purely and simply, and not try to justify it by reasoning and quoting authorities, as in doing so he would simply be trying to impress the client with his scholarliness and intelligence. This and other remarks about decorum are often delightful.

There is no end of sound advice, as modern as can be, in Artemidorus' *Oneirocritica,* but it requires close philological scrutiny. Artemidorus makes difficult reading, especially since a good edition of this text did not exist before 1963,[31] and no reliable translation had emerged before 1979.[32] This may account for the fact that most modern psychologists turn up their noses at him, in spite of the fact that Freud has taken quite some trouble to discuss him. But even with Freud, strangely enough, Artemidorus did not stick. He had apparently to hurry on to develop his own

30 Sophocles, *Frag.* 704 (ed. A. Nauck [Leipzig, 1889]).
31 Artemiodori Daldiani, *Oneirocriticon Libri V.*, ed. Roger A. Pack (Leipzig, 1963).
32 Artemidor von Daldis, *Das Traumbuch,* trans. Karl Brackertz (Zürich, 1979).

new ideas, which were indeed shattering enough, so that we can well understand that he got completely wrapped up in them.

II.

Incubation seems to me to be only one example of something you will notice at once when you go to Greece: the whole country is imbued with myth even today. All the old gods are still alive. And if you take a map of the country in one hand and Pausanias' "Baedeker" (if possible in Frazer's edition with commentary[33]) in the other, you will soon realize that what you are actually looking at is the geography of the human soul. Not the Greek, not the Western, but the human soul, *tout court*. Spread over the peninsula and its islands are hundreds of places each of which has its special myth, its cult and cult-legends, and sanctuaries, each of which would take care of one or another of the most basic problems of human life in the most varied, complete, beautiful and healing way. If you had been in need of help in those days, you would have known exactly where to go to find enacted for you the appropriate archetype.

33 Pausanias, *Description of Greece* (trans. and with commentary, J.G. Frazer [London, 1913]).

EPICRISIS
FOR THE THINKING READER

WHAT HAVE ANCIENT HEALING CULTS to do with modern psychology? In antiquity anyone dedicating himself to the cult of a particular deity was called a *therapeutēs*. This is what doctors claim to be. Later, in Hellenistic and early Christian times, some ascetics called themselves therapists without assigning any medical meaning to the term. This points to the close relation between cult and cure in antiquity.

But is modern psychotherapy a cult? This accusation has been raised against Jungian analytical psychology all too often. Even more it is accused of being an esoteric secret society. Any examination of Jung's tremendous opus shows that, perhaps more than any other great man of our profession, he labored unremittingly to describe and elaborate the results of his research and practice. Truly Jung's work is not willfully mysterious or esoteric. Anyone is of course free to believe this superstition and put Jung on his private Index.

Jung has empirically discovered something which offers a close point of contact with the ancient healing cults. He has established these two facts:

1. The human psyche has an autochthonous spiritual function.
2. No patient in the second half of life has been cured without that patient's finding an approach to this spiritual function.

It might be assumed that, after such findings, theologians would have flocked to Jung's consulting room; but this has not happened. Naturally, theologians may not need this healing. But they might at least be glad that an experimentally proved *theolo-*

gia naturalis exists. Why does such a reaction fail to occur? The problem is not simple, and the answer, too, varies. But for the medical psychologist Jung's results are most interesting, if only because they are highly relevant to his professional work. Morbid symptoms give the immediate impression of remoteness from God. This idea is expressed in the German language when one inquires about the nature of an illness by asking, "Was fehlt Ihnen?" ("What do you lack?") In the Greek and Roman Asclepieia the answer given was entirely unambiguous, since the healing consisted in some epiphany of the god in any one of his forms, in a waking vision or a dream. Whatever the patient "lacked" was thereupon obviously integrated and the cure was completed.

But if a cure, at least in the field of neurosis, depends upon the recognition of the spiritual function of the soul, then the conclusion may be drawn that it is remoteness from God which is the *causa* for the effect termed "neurosis." The reintroduction of the spiritual function would then serve as causal therapy. In other words, what many of Jung's patients "lacked" was exactly this spiritual function and its conscious recognition. This explanation can be called a logically and philosophically inadmissible simplification or generalization. The comparison is applicable only in the relatively infrequent cases in which substitution therapy (as it is called in medicine) is indicated (diabetes/insulin). The real situation is usually much more complicated.

If, for instance, there is even a grain of truth in Freud's concept that the genesis of neurosis has its source in early infantile conflicts, there remains little room for a spiritual etiology. From this perspective, at least, it is easy to understand why Freud could not reach the same conclusions Jung did. But in dealing with neuroses and psychic disturbances does a causal-etiological inquiry suffice, or indeed has it any meaning? For, if a lack or deficiency of the spiritual element is not what causes the disease, as must be the case when the Freudian causal mechanisms appear adequate, and yet, according to Jung, a correction or substitution in this regard is a *conditio sine qua non* for a cure, the causal-reductive approach does not go very far. The ensuing cure can be explained only by the assumption that the whole system of patient, illness and doctor has in the course of the treatment undergone a certain transformation of meaning and that this has made a solution of the problem possible. This solution would also accomplish something not simply corresponding to a regression into the past but something in effect completely new. It might be tempting to infer that the whole neurotic or psychotic interval was designed from the outset just to lead the patient to accept the demands of religion. Herewith the sickness itself would be explained as essentially unreal and would be almost degraded to a neurotic arrangement in the sense of A. Adler. The problem of *motive,* however, could not be fitted into Adler's all-embracing explanation of the drive to power. What other unconscious complex then could be behind it? If this complex is disclosed only with the cure, at the end of a usually prolonged effort called analysis, it must certainly have been really unconscious, not just repressed or forgotten. Hence it cannot be deduced from anything already known. Consequently it would be methodologically false, after Jung's discoveries, to begin an analytic treatment from the beginning with the fixed intention of wresting at any cost this unconscious spiritual factor, like the Manichaean spark of light, from the darkness of unconscious matter. Such a *petitio principii* would be the wrong approach for many reasons. Any analyst with such a monotonous prejudice could never do justice to the manifold diversity of his patients. Whoever operates with a panacea fails to be an analyst; by this procedure he only demonstrates the reality of his own monomania. He is possessed by a complex which he perforce injects into the interpretation of every one of his cases.

Nothing is as firmly based on subjective conviction as the spiritual element. If the patient needs it for his cure, he must discover it by himself, in himself, it may be said to his own great astonishment, as the result of his most personal research and effort. And the analyst may do no more than cautiously accompany the patient or, at the most, guide him.

In a successful cure the system must have undergone a transformation of meaning during the process of the illness and treatment; that is, the spiritual element was not an original component of the illness but a product of it, and eventually of the treatment as well. It is true that to the spiritual attitude every sickness, like every stroke of fate, has always seemed inflicted by God and thus part of His preordained plan of salvation. This holds also when it seems to be a matter of punishment only.

This finalism is preferable to the blind compulsion of the stars, at least wherever the stars are no longer gods. The god in question seems to have a dubious role, for it is he who makes men sick. Yahweh sent illness, and then later Apollo, and, at least till the Baroque period, the God of Christians. A psychologically significant variation on this theme is the god of healing who is himself sick or wounded. Also very closely connected with this idea is poison as a healing remedy, or the healing effect of the weapon that wounded Wagner's Parsifal. Today the idea of a disease-inflicting god no longer seems attractive. But these mythologems are not merely priestly fraud, on the pattern of "God made you sick; believe and in gratitude he will make you well again." Nowadays patients seem to show better results if the suspicion is voiced that the illness may in some way be their own fault. But this is true only for patients already somewhat "enlightened" – intellectuals and rationalists – for at bottom this is a purely causal concept. But if, as Jung has said, healing depends on a successful connection with the spiritual element and it is not a mere substitution, then the simple relation between *causa morbi,* cause of illness, and remedy no longer exists. From the "mental hygiene" point of view this is good. For if the patient were able to make himself sick as well as healthy, he would be on a par with those gods possessing these particular attributes. He would then by this godlikeness risk adding the danger – not to be underestimated – of adding delusions of grandeur to his existing neurosis.

Where now has this discussion led? Through the ages a number of views or theories regarding the "whence and whither" of diseases have been offered. A purely etiological-causal analysis of neuroses and psychoses does not provide particularly satisfactory results. Therapy, much less a cure, does not eventuate. Granted the correctness of Jung's observations, there can be no cure unless the patient succeeds in forming a relation to a newly added element, religion. However, remoteness from God must not be unconditionally regarded as a component in the genesis of a neurosis or psychosis. If this were so, spiritual people would not develop such disturbances. Rather, the remoteness must be realized at some point in the illness, so that the lack becomes felt and help can be found, according to Jung's prescription. It sometimes happens that a person hit by such an illness will for the first time feel himself alienated from God. Witness Job or the melancholia of King Saul (I Sam. 28:15 "… and God is departed from me, and answereth me no more, neither by prophets, nor by dreams.") How this help is brought about, or rather the way it happens, cannot be described here and is in any case an extremely complicated subject. Jung, in all his longer works – at least since the Terry Lectures in 1937 – delineates this process. However, the answer to the question is hinted at in the first of the two statements by Jung cited earlier: that it is possible to demonstrate the existence of a natural spiritual function in the human psyche.

The question arises, How does Jung define healing? Unfortunately he does not define it explicitly, but it is clear from many passages in his works that he does not mean the healing of symptoms. Symptoms are healed every day in the offices of doctors of all sorts, and are set down as cured by doctor and patient alike, whether the result meets Jung's criteria or not. Neurotic symptoms, too, disappear on occasion, because of, or in spite of, every kind of therapy or nontherapy. Jung has in mind the goal of leading the patient to understand the meaning of his life, of his suffering, of his being what he is. With this insight would surely come a well-established spiritual attitude, and the result would be not merely a remission but a real cure, which could also be called a transformation.

The goal can be formulated in another way. The illness is creatively reshaped by successfully combatting it and incorporating it meaningfully into the totality of the patient's life, with the patient really understanding and learning the lesson. Only then will danger of a relapse be avoided.

But this goal is an achievement not easily attained. The illness must yield a meaning. This is the age-old pious concept that behind the sickness a meaning lies hidden which demands recognition – philosophically, the *causa finalis*.

Every psychiatrist required to seek the meaning of illness calls to mind the impressive heaping up of obvious nonsense in regard to neuroses and psychoses. Freud founded modern psychology by explaining all this nonsense in terms of neurotic symptoms, faulty behavior and dreams. Jung then undertook with the same success to demonstrate the hidden meaning in schizophrenic neologisms (e.g., "I am the Lorelei" in *Psychologie der Dementia praecox,* 1907). But even today, though the key to this peculiar code has been found, it is as yet not clear what forces these patients to express themselves so bizarrely, so that the basic meaning of these strange manifestations still remains obscure. With slightly more success we have turned to the wider problem of the possible meaning of psychoses in general. The word "meaning" is here equivalent to "function," the function of bringing to consciousness predominantly collective-unconscious material. The problem of meaning also relates to the possibilities of cure and of a possible therapy. This therapy would be equivalent to a constructive redeployment of the previously destructive demons and would result in a totally changed situation from the premorbid initial condition. Here "meaning" has something to do with a *telos* and is to a large extent identical with the quest for a *causa finalis*. Jung has suggested that schizophrenia can be seen as "a gigantic attempt at compensation" on the part of the unconscious, a compensation for the narrowness of consciousness, or, as he once said, of the *Weltanschauung*. In line with what Jung has said concerning the cure of neuroses, the diagnosis of a cure, too, is rarely reached unless the *telos* of including the spiritual element is reached at the same time. In spite of a great deal of discussion nowadays about analytic treatment and the cure of schizophrenics, this criterion is not mentioned. Everyone seems to be still satisfied with the causal-reductive interpretation of the results. I myself have had experience in analyzing only two schizophrenics, and that as far back as the early thirties, when there was as yet no talk of the analytic therapy of schizophrenia.

> One of these patients provides an example in brief: He was still a young man, a severe catatonic, confined in the clinic for years. When I took over the section for disturbed patients, where he was at the time, my predecessor warned me of his reputed aggressiveness, which had made him generally feared. On this occasion the patient was standing almost cataleptically in a corner of the dayroom. The following day I looked at him more closely and noticed that, in contrast to the general impression he gave, there was in his eyes something alive and humanly warm. I immediately walked up to him and extended my hand. To my considerable surprise he silently pressed my hand in return. The next day I took him to my office, causing some excitement among the attendants. Once there, the patient began to talk at great speed. In the following sessions he explained his whole delusional system. This is not the place to go into detail, but the patient was normalized in the course of two weeks, and after another two weeks, was discharged from the clinic. Nine years later I met him by accident on the street, where he introduced his financée to me. A brief catamnesis showed that since his discharge from the clinic he had worked without interruption and that there was little danger of a relapse. He took leave of me, saying: "Yes, indeed, doctor, if one hadn't experienced it, one would never believe how much good could come from such an illness." His expression as he spoke left no room for doubt that the years in the Burghölzli Clinic had been transmuted into a really spiritual, deep experience which

had healed this man, had made him whole. He had therefore become a *religiosus,* which represents an advantage arising from illness (*Krankheitsgewinn*) in its most literal sense.

Single cases lack all statistical significance, no matter how impressive they are. Just because they are impressive, their general significance can easily be overvalued. To achieve a broader basis, we must seek analogous experiences in related fields and so place the single case in a larger context, though without committing a *metabasis eis allo genos* (shift to another topic).

1. A belief that the meaning of an illness may be closely connected with its cure recalls the ancient mythologem *ho trōsas iasetai,* "The wounder heals" (oracle of Apollo cited by Apollodorus). Here the sickness is unequivocally given the dignity of a remedy, just as poison is a medicine and vice versa. The principle for various reasons is carried so far that the patient becomes the healer and the physician becomes sick.

2. According to the ancient theory, the two concepts *nosos* (illness) and *penia* (poverty) cannot be separated any more than *hygieia* (health) and *ploutos* (wealth) can be. So sickness is equivalent to poverty, and health to riches. He who is ill certainly feels a "lack" (*penia*) of something (as is expressed in the German *fehlt*), while he who is well possesses plenty, or wholeness (*ploutos*).

3. Consequently, the mythological realm knows only one possibility of healing, that is, when the god who is himself sick or wounded intervenes personally. This is clearly the case in the Asclepieia. It must be stressed that no medical treatment was given, although according to extant case histories there were often overt organic changes. The procedure is exclusively irrational. Causal therapy does not exist; in place of the principle of causality we find that of analogy, the *similia similibus curantur* ("like is cured by like") which later becomes familiar in homeopathy (poison = remedy).

4. This remedy is known only to the god of healing, and the

requisite intervention is carried out by him alone (in a dream), and with this the treatment is complete. So the cure consists in a divine intercession, in other words, in the advent of a personified divine principle. The patient displays his recognition of this fact by a votive offering in the temple, that of Asclepius, for instance, and remains bound to the god as a *religiosus*.

These old principles are still valid in psychic illnesses and disturbances if we keep in mind Jung's two statements and the experiences in the psychiatric clinic that I described. The concurring voices through many centuries speak for themselves. Jung's theories stem from the vast material at his disposal. This he has collected with special attention to those processes in the unconscious, above all in dreams, which parallel the difficulties in the conscious. If the patient succeeds in coming consciously to terms with these unconscious processes, two different results can be demonstrated:

1. A development can be shown which ends with the patient gaining access to religion, or a connection with it. (Jung's point 2; see beginning of this chapter).
2. The parallelism just mentioned between conscious and unconscious is more like an antiparallelism. Here Jung uses the expression "compensation." By this he means that the unconscious products counteract inadequate or false conscious ideas, and if the import of the unconscious can be raised to the conscious level, a balance can be achieved.

Both these facts have been discovered empirically and can be convincingly proved. Also they meet the test as heuristic principles in daily practice. But the compensatory function of unconscious phenomena in relation to those of consciousness requires closer theoretical research. This relation might be likened to regulatory circuits as they occur in automation. "Self-regulatory systems" can be used as a model for certain biological regulations. But even within the area of conscious functions, we reach the point where "feedback" is no longer a sufficient explanation.

The founder of cybernetics, Norbert Wiener, makes this clear enough in his book *The Human Use of Human Beings* (London, 1950). Still less does the cybernetic model suffice to explain the relation of the conscious to the unconscious – quite aside from its failure to give even the most rudimentary idea of the nature of the communicating channels.

Of course, when ill, the patient "lacks something," and so it might easily be thought that this deficiency could be corrected by the self-regulatory processes of the psyche. But such a psychic process would be quantitative, complementing and not compensating. A complement is equivalent to an answer to a problem that in principle one is able to solve, either by sufficient knowledge or sufficient time, or by having available a professional (e.g., an analyst) who knows the answer. This is mainly the case with psychological problems resolved according to Freud or Adler. Here a widespread misconception regarding Adler's theory should be countered. It is customary to describe it as teleologically oriented. For example, the "advantage" arising from the illness explains the illness and "sanctifies" it as purposive. The successfully analyzed patient loses his fictional goals and false solutions and, with them, the neurosis. In other words, the correct solution comes as "output" from the computer, whose programmer is called analyst, in contrast to the false programming produced by the patient before analysis and backed up by his neurosis. The Adlerian concept is not really teleological, for the correct answer was from the outset in the system itself; the ego simply did not want to know it, preferring a false one. On the other hand, this situation seems to be pretty well covered by the cybernetic model. Philosophically speaking, Adler's system is rather an *immanent* teleology, for which the principle of regulatory systems is adequate.

But Jung's concept of compensation must be unconditionally ascribed to a *transcendent* teleology. To be sure, the logical application of his statement that the manifestations of the unconscious have compensatory significance also leads to a "feedback" which changes both the conscious and the unconscious. This gives rise to what Jung called the process of individuation. This event, as is shown empirically, has a *telos* which one would never have imputed to either the neurosis or its host. But this *telos* can be symbolically prefigured before it comes to realization and, by the use of analogies, it can be seen to encompass a totality, the totality of the human personality. "Whole" and "healed" are synonymous; he who is healed has become whole. Both qualities, as Jung teaches, are related to the spiritual function; and experience shows that this function arises spontaneously with the appearance of the symbols of totality. Retrospectively the *telos* becomes a *causa finalis* – one, however, which could never have been found without the consistent use of the theory of compensation. Spiritual phenomena and cure are practically identical and are felt subjectively as transcendent, that is, as a new element which was not originally a part, no matter how hidden, of the system itself. Consequently, no one was in a position to foresee the answer. Thus this conclusion leads to a complete agreement with the clinical findings of antiquity: divine intercession is equivalent to healing.

There are unfortunately no simple solutions for these infinitely difficult problems. These many meanderings, hopefully cautious and open-minded, are attempts to circumambulate them.

Final causation presupposes absolute knowledge or foreknowledge – certainly a theoretical *aporia* (a bottomless uncertainty) of the first order. What is more, physicians are empiricists, and empiricists are generally known to be antimetaphysical. But what if empiricism, and that means causalism, compels admission of final causes? The *consensus gentium* has already lent them a certain probability, as shown by the ancient concepts in regard to sickness and cure. In psychiatry the senselessness of phenomena is more impressive than in somatic medicine. This makes the problem of meaning even more intriguing. It is indeed a practical problem, for its solution will mean for the patient that the "plan for salvation" has been found. There is method in this senselessness, but, it must be kept in mind, a method impossible to discern or understand beforehand.

It must be stressed that even after this understanding is achieved, the secret remains a secret; for where does man stand in relation to the problem of meaning? Far beyond any professional viewpoint, it really appears as if the "whole enormous nonsense" existed solely to force man to find in it the sense or plan of healing, and this not in psychiatry alone.

The search for an answer has produced various suggestions. To give only one example: according to Poseidonius, the problem of purpose belongs to theology, since it assumes a particular force, a *logikē dynamis,* a power of reason, and therefore has nothing to do with physics. Poseidonius also speaks of a *zōtikē dynamis,* translated by Cicero, with his usual correctness, as *vis vitalis* ("vital force"). This of course, as you can see, does not mean the same thing as vitalism. But what are final causes? If final causes exist and even become observable after one understands the whole *quid pro quo,* and if, then, this absolute knowledge is a fact, who is it that has started all this and confused it in such subtle and complicated ways? Admittedly this question contains a concealed anthropomorphism. But does that make it a projection? Religions both in the Old Testament and during classical times attributed *pronoia* (foreknowledge) to the divine.

Or is it also mere anthropomorphism to conclude that this absolute knowledge has a subject (a knower that knows it)? But this is to introduce unintentionally an argument for the existence of God and that through the experiences of psychology. The problem seems to appertain rather to Eckhart's question whether "God has not yet become world."

At Lourdes the modern motto is *per Mariam ad Jesum.* The virginal immaculate conception leads to the Son-God or Son of God, who is the Anthropos, the whole man. The pre-existent totality is achieved, with the Mother who is a virgin as mediator. The analogies to Hygieia and Asclepius are striking. Those familiar with Jung's presentations of the individuation process will also note the analogy to his phenomenology.

In reply to the question as to what are the consequences of all these observations as far as the modern doctor is concerned, there are just as many answers and further questions as there are doctors; so each one must come to terms with this in his own way, for in a modern practice such wonderful healing dreams are few and far between. This seems to be mainly due to the fact that we are not in a position to create the atmosphere conducive to such phenomena. This applies to the somatically as well as the psychologically oriented clinic. A second factor can be traced to the tradition that the patient must be imbued with a faith in a Savior God, a role which the modern therapist cannot do full justice to. Whether or not the transference phenomenon is helpful in this respect is a moot point, for it calls for superhuman qualities in the doctor and involves the risk of inflation. In English another word for doctor is "physician." This leads us to the conclusion that, in view of all the facts depicted above, every physician would also have to be a metaphysician.

List of Abbreviations

AHW: Otto Weinreich, "Antike Heilungswunder: Untersuchungen zum Wunderglauben der Griechen und Römer," *RGVV,* VIII (1909), I.

CIL: *Corpus Inscriptionum Latinarum.*

ERE: *Encyclopaedia of Religion and Ethics,* ed. James Hastings (Edinburgh, 1908-1926).

Frazer, *Pausanias: Pausanias's Description of Greece.* Translated, with commentary, by J.G. Frazer (6 vols.; London, 1913).

Gruppe, *Handbuch:* O. Gruppe, "Griechische Mythologie und Religionsgeschichte," *Handbuch der klassischen Altertumswissenschaft,* ed. Iwan von Müller (Munich, 1906), V, 2, I and II.

Herzog, *Kos: Archaeologisches Institut des deutschen Reiches: Kos. Ergebnisse der deutschen Ausgrabungen und Forschungen,* ed. Rudolf Herzog (Berlin, 1932). Vol. I: *Asklepieion.*

Herzog, "Heilige Gesetze von Kos": *Abhandlungen der preussischen Akademie der Wissenschaften, Phil-hist. Klasse,* No. 6 (Berlin, 1928).

IG: *Inscriptiones Graecae.*

Kern, *Religion:* O. Kern, *Die Religion der Griechen* (3 vols.; Berlin, 1926-1938).

P.-W.: *Realencyclopaedie der classischen Altertumswissenschaft,* ed. Pauly, Wissowa and Kroll (Stuttgart, 1894-1983).

Preller-Robert, *Griechische Mythologie: Griechische Mythologie von L. Preller,* ed. Carl Robert (2 vols; 4th ed. Berlin, 1894-1926).

RGVV: *Religionsgeschichtliche Versuche und Vorarbeiten,* founded by Albrecht Dieterich and Richard Wünsch, ed. R. Wünsch and Ludwig Deubner (Giessen, 1903 – Berlin, 1939 seq.).

Roscher, *Lexikon: Ausführliches Lexikon der griechischen und römischen Mythologie,* ed. W.H. Roscher (Leipzig, 1884-1937).

Samter: Ernst Samter, *Die Religion der Griechen* ("Natur und Geisteswelt," No. 457) (Leipzig, 1914).

WHE: Rudolf Herzog, "Die Wunderheilungen von Epidauros," *Philologus* (Leipzig, 1931), Supplement XXII, 3.

Wissowa, *Kult:* Georg Wissowa, "Religion und Kultus der Römer," *Handbuch der klassischen Altertumswissenschaft,* ed. Iwan von Müller (Munich, 1912), V, 4.

TABLE OF DREAMS, ORACLES AND VISIONS FROM ANTIQUITY

(modern dreams in subject index)

(Iamata numbers refer to inscriptions at Epidaurus)

INDEX OF NAMES

a) Places

(See also sites of Asclepieia, oracles, and temples in subject index)

b) Ancient Persons and Authors

c) More Recent Persons and Authors

INDEX OF SUBJECTS

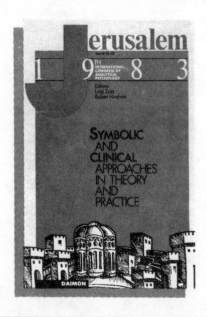

ENGLISH PUBLICATIONS BY **DAIMON**

The Savage and Beautiful Country, Alan McGlashan
A Testament to the Wilderness, Ed. by R. Hinshaw
Talking with Angels, (transcribed by Gitta Mallasz)
A Time to Mourn, Verena Kast
Imprints of the Future, George Czuczka
Healing Dream and Ritual, C.A. Meier
Meetings with Jung, E.A. Bennet
Life Paints its own Span, Susan Bach
Hermes and his Children, Rafael López-Pedraza
Cultural Anxiety, Rafael López-Pedraza
Jungian Psychiatry, Heinrich K. Fierz
The Myth of Meaning, Aniela Jaffé
Was C.G. Jung a Mystic? Aniela Jaffé
From the Life and Work of C.G. Jung, Aniela Jaffé
Friedrich Nietzsche, L. Frey-Rohn

Jungian Congress Papers:

Jerusalem 1983: *Symbolic and Clinical Approaches*
Ed. by Luigi Zoja, R. Hinshaw

Berlin 1986: *The Archetypal Shadow in a Split World*
Ed. by M.-A. Mattoon

Available from your bookstore or from our distributors:

Worldwide
Daimon Verlag
Am Klosterplatz
CH-8840 Einsiedeln
Switzerland
Tel. (55) 53 22 66

Great Britain
Element Books Ltd.
Longmead Shaftesbury
Dorset SP7 8PL
England
Tel. (0747) 51339

USA
Sigo Press
25 New Chardon St. # 8748
Boston, MA 02114
Tel. (617) 523 2321

USA West
The Great Tradition
750 Adrian Way, Suite 111
San Rafael, CA 94903
Tel. (415) 492 9382